Does this PEN WORK

HURST MEMORIAL LIBRARY
Pacific Christian College
2500 E. Nutwood
 CA. 92631

Not very well

Measuring the Church Growth Movement

Measuring the Church Growth Movement

By
J. ROBERTSON McQUILKIN

MOODY PRESS
CHICAGO

Originally entitled
How Biblical Is the Church Growth Movement?

© 1973, 1974, by
THE MOODY BIBLE INSTITUTE
OF CHICAGO

Revised Edition

ISBN: 0-8024-5219-1

Printed in the United States of America

CONTENTS

CHAPTER		PAGE
	FOREWORD	7
	INTRODUCTION	9
1.	NUMBERS *Is numerical church growth a most crucial task in missions?*	19
2.	SELECTIVITY *Is it right for the church to concentrate on the responsive elements of society?*	34
3.	CONVERSION *Are people movement conversions valid?*	44
4.	SCIENCE *Are anthropological studies legitimate for evangelism?*	50
5.	PROPHECY *Will large growth result from using Church Growth principles and techniques?*	67
	CONCLUSION	73
	APPENDIX	77
	NOTES	84
	BIBLIOGRAPHY	86

FOREWORD

The Church Growth Movement should appeal primarily to mission-minded evangelicals. Yet there have been skeptics, even among the leaders of this group. In part it has been based on misunderstanding. But even more, some have wondered if this teaching comes from the Bible.

For this reason it is very timely that the present penetrating study should appear. It bears special weight, coming from an outsider to the movement, who has had invaluable experience as a missionary in the difficult field of Japan, and who now heads an important school of missionary training. The specific topics discussed are well chosen and cover the most basic questions. The author examines very carefully five basic presuppositions of the movement. He defines the theological issues involved and in each section lists both the strengths and the weaknesses of the Church Growth position.

It is a discriminating and well balanced treatment that deserves careful study by both mission leaders and prospective missionaries.

HAROLD R. COOK

INTRODUCTION

BIBLICAL AUTHORITY AND CHURCH GROWTH

Is Church Growth thinking biblical thinking? Can a movement born of scientific observation and spread through the enthusiastic promotion of dynamic leadership be biblically valid?

A pragmatic, rapidly growing movement may not pause long enough to articulate its basic presuppositions, let alone challenge their validity. It is the purpose of this book to isolate the basic theological presuppositions of the Church Growth Movement and to examine their biblical validity.

Why is it necessary for a demonstrably successful method to be analyzed and interrogated in the light of Scripture? Is not its very success an adequate self-validation?

No, is the answer given by two widely divergent opponents of Church Growth thinking. Those represented by the dominant leadership of the World Council of Churches oppose Church Growth teaching because of its view of the mission of the church. These opponents are the strongest critics. The confrontation is outlined in chapter one. For these churchmen and missiologists who reject Church Growth's view of the mission of the church there is no real debate with the other presuppositions discussed in these lectures—they are either irrelevant or quite acceptable. For this reason, most of our consideration will be the confrontation with the other opponents of Church Growth, those who are of evangelical persuasion.

It is chiefly evangelicals, whether opponents, advocates, or neutral toward Church Growth theory, to whom these pages are addressed. I could hope that the nonevangelical would read at least chapter one, for there we deal with the issue in which he is vitally interested. But chiefly I address the evangelical. I do this because four out of the five issues in the debate are of interest primarily to those who have accepted the first Church Growth thesis, that numerical church growth is a crucial task in missions.

And this is no insignificant audience. It is the evangelical branch that is doing most of the missionary work of the church today. Probably seventy-five percent of the mission force today is being sent abroad by Christians who believe that the Bible is the authoritative and infallible Word of God. Missionary societies with a high view of Scripture are flourishing. Missionary societies which hold low views of Scripture are declining.

For those who constitute the bulk of my audience, then, any spiritual idea or activity not in harmony with the Bible is only apparently successful and is unsuccessful in reality. Thus by determining, insofar as possible, whether an idea or activity is or is not compatible with the Word of God, the one committed to this authority may know in advance whether or not he is pleasing God and whether or not he is eligible for success on God's terms.

"All Scripture is inspired by God and is useful for teaching the truth, rebuking error, correcting fault, and giving instruction for right living, so that the man who serves God may be fully qualified and equipped to do every kind of good work" (2 Ti 3:16, paraphrase). Some who hold the Bible as the ultimate authority do not agree that the Bible is infallible. This book may well prove of equal value to them because they also are vitally concerned that all the faith, life, and work of the Christian actually conform to the Word of God. But I should state at the outset my conviction that the link between authority and infallibility is essential.

Introduction

Any word derives its authority from its source. We say that the source of the Bible is God and thus it has ultimate authority. But for the Bible to have any independent authority as a word from God, it must be all from God. Otherwise one's actual authority will not be the Bible itself, but rather the basis on which the choice is made as to which part one considers from God and which from man. Thus the teaching of an inerrant Scripture is the great continental divide in theology—not the most important doctrine to be sure, but the most crucial. For no matter what evangelical doctrines one stoutly defends, when error in the Scripture is admitted, the authority has shifted at that point to the person or principles that decide what is in error and what is not in error. For example, some would accept the authority of Scripture in theological or religious areas but not in historical matters. But what is the criterion for distinguishing between history and theology? Is creation an historical problem or is it theological? And what of the resurrection? The Word of God written must stand in independent judgment upon what we believe and disbelieve and on how we behave.

But loyal adherence to the doctrine of an inerrant Word does not guarantee that one's mission activities or program has actually been brought under the authority of that Word. The allegiance may indeed be to a constitutional monarchy in which actual control is vested elsewhere than in the monarch. The purpose of this book will be to suggest how the Bible itself should be in functional control when we adopt, modify, or reject any of the ideas advocated by people associated with the Church Growth Movement.

To say that the Bible is our authority does not mean that all Scripture is of equal authority in determining the will of God for His people today. This is especially true when we seek to know that portion of His will which concerns church growth. Some of God's will is clearly prescribed in Scripture, but not all. For example, *what* God wants done is clearly prescribed.

The objectives of evangelism and the content of the message are in this category. Although some of the *how* is clearly prescribed (you must organize as a church whether or not you like organization), much of the method is not clearly spelled out.

A great deal of the *how* is defined by principles. Some of these principles are obvious—they lie close to the surface of Bible teaching. The principle that the church is God's means for accomplishing His purposes in world evangelization is one such obvious principle. Other principles which are not so obvious must be mined and refined. For example, are anthropological studies for church growth biblically valid? Should the church concentrate on the responsive elements of society? These are ideas on which biblical principles certainly impinge, but not in a direct and obvious way.

The Bible does not speak at all of some elements of method either by direct prescription or in clear principle. Sometimes the missionary is to find the will of God in a situation through direct leading of the Holy Spirit. For example, the early missionary band experienced a very halting discovery of the will of God. In Acts 16 Paul's gospel team made two false starts before discovering the direction they were actually to go. Perhaps they were drawn by large opportunity or driven by past experience. But God guided them by His Spirit in an unexpected path.

At other times, God's servant is left to his own discretion. "If ye be disposed" (1 Co 10;27), the apostle said, leaving the choice to the Christian's judgment, or even to his preference.

Sometimes these two—the voice of the Spirit and one's own judgment—are difficult to distinguish from one another. But in neither case do such methods or activities have the authority of the Word of God. Personal judgment must be held lightly, ready for change. Ideas not revealed in Scripture, when pressed on others with dogmatism, undermine the authority of the Word of God.

Introduction

When we speak of bringing Church Growth theses under the authority of the Word of God, we are looking for three distinct kinds of validity: first, those matters which are clearly prescribed in Scripture; then, matters which, though not clearly prescribed, are required because of clear biblical principle; and, finally, those areas which lack such authority, having been derived from human experience and insight, but which are nevertheless compatible with biblical teaching.

Are we on a search, then, for prooftexts, either to document each concept or to invalidate it? Are we ferreting out biblical examples that seem to be analogous to Church Growth concepts, pro and con? Though documentation and illustration are necessary and helpful, the method of bringing any theological teaching or presupposition under the authority of Scripture is much more profound than that. The hermeneutical principles necessary for building any Bible doctrine will be used in examining the theological presuppositions of the Church Growth Movement.

In developing the program of the church, *all biblical requirements must be included*. To say that all scriptural teaching concerning church growth must be followed by the church, is not to say that every missionary nor every segment of the church is responsible to fulfill all the requirements of Scripture. Specialization is valid. For example, in the evangelistic responsibility of the church, Pacific Broadcasting Association may have special responsibilty for *proclamation*, Billy Graham may have special responsibility for *persuasion*, and the Medical Assistance Program may be particularly concerned with "presence evangelism," demonstrating the love of God by deeds of mercy. But the church as a whole and any local congregation is responsible to see that all of the prescribed responsibilities are fulfilled.

If a group or individual has a specialized ministry, he must be careful not to give the impression that his ministry is the whole of the church's responsibility. He must contribute his part humbly in the context of the whole church's obedience to *all* the authoritative Word of God. Therefore if the Church Growth Movement does not incorporate all Bible concepts concerning the growth of the church, it may yet be valid as a specialization, caring for a select aspect of biblical responsibility. But to be valid as a specialization, it must be self-consciously so—that is, it must contribute the specialization in terms of relating it biblically to the whole Bible truth on the subject. For if it gives the impression of totality while being in fact only partial, the practical result will be in violation of this first principle for biblical interpretation of doctrine: *All* scriptural teaching on the subject must be incorporated.

If any of the prescribed ingredients are left out by the church, the result will not be mere failure to succeed. It may well be destructive. Not only will the medicine so compounded not effect a cure, it may well prove to be poison bringing injury or death to the patient. So it is with widely prescribed "cures" for the world's ills that are compounded solely of concern for men's bodies and societies, leaving out the active ingredients of salvation from sin and reconciliation with God. They will not merely fail in effecting the cure, their prescription is poison and will ultimately destroy multitudes. How do sincere churchmen write such prescriptions? By failing to be subject to the authoritative Word of God which prescribes *all* the necessary ingredients.

In developing the program of the church, *only biblical requirements may be used authoritatively*. Methods, activities, ideas not specifically expressed in Scripture may certainly be utilized in the program of the church. But such additives must be compatible with biblically prescribed ingredients. Further, since extrabiblical methods lack divine authority, they may not be imposed on others. If an added ingredient dilutes, neutralizes, or counteracts any biblically prescribed ingredient, it is not acceptable.

For example, false motivation such as bribery is not compatible with biblical evangelism. Force and violence are antithetic to biblical principles for effecting God's purposes through the church. Even such innocent procedures as "indigenous principles" derived from the use of the book of Acts as a rigid blueprint, when vested with authority as the will of God, have at times inhibited the effectiveness of other biblical ingredients in evangelistic church-starting.

In developing the program of the church, *the Bible's own emphases must be maintained.* The right proportion of biblical ingredients is necessary—the biblical mix is important. The danger of any specialized supplier of certain services is that the emphasis of Scripture may become unbalanced and, again, not only is a cure unlikely, but often poison is disseminated under a thoroughly biblical label.

For example, proclamation evangelism has been the sole mission of certain groups. I have known such groups which go into a community and give a ten-minute address in the doorway of each home. At the end of the address is a warning that salvation will come to those who leave all and follow (the team) or else there will be judgment. Following the proclamation to one person in each house of a community, the group moves on. Not only did God's will go unaccomplished, but great harm was done to many people and to the cause of Christ.

Again, some groups overemphasize presence evangelism, while others underemphasize it, each receiving the results which always come to those who do not rigorously and vigorously bring every aspect of the program to the bar of the authoritative Word of God.

These, then, are the three questions we shall seek to ask about each of the Church Growth presuppositions:

1. Is *all* scriptural teaching on the subject reflected in each presupposition? Is all scriptural teaching on the subject of church growth included in the program? If not, is that which is included in the program adequately related to

those elements of Bible teaching on the subject which are purposefully left out?
2. Are the extrabiblical contributions in harmony with Scripture, and are they held to a secondary status without divine authority? In other words, is Scripture *alone* the ultimate authority?
3. Are the biblical *emphases* maintained?

In this way, the chapters that follow will seek to determine to what extent the basic Church Growth theses are biblically valid.

The movement has not always been self-consciously theological. It is now becoming so, but historically it has been a pragmatic movement with certain theological presuppositions gradually refined. It seems to have begun with the presupposition that one way for large church growth is multi-individual, interdependent decision. Coupled with this was the idea that a chief task in missions is numerical church growth and the assumption that the pattern of people movements could be duplicated through careful planning. Dr. McGavran's message in *The Bridges of God* that the old mission station approach should be replaced by the people movement approach was often misinterpreted to mean group conversion,[1] so in subsequent publications he has stressed that the concept is multi-individual conversion. The evangelistic goal is not merely individuals, but individuals as means or bridges to all their family, clan, or tribe, with the group moving together toward Christ.

In 1959 McGavran published *How Churches Grow*. A strong emphasis of this book is that the church should concentrate its resources on the responsive. This was misinterpreted by many as meaning that the church should not try to reach the unresponsive at all. Subsequent articles and books by McGavran have sought to clarify this misunderstanding.

At any rate, these basic assumptions had profound theolog-

Introduction

ical implications, and because of these theological implications, the controversy has been churchwide, involving opposition from those who understand the implications and from those who do not, both from liberal and conservative camps, though for widely varying reasons.

In my own experience as a missionary seeking to do the will of God, I had reached certain conclusions advocated by the Church Growth Movement before I heard of it. For example, I had come to the conclusion that I would concentrate on the responsive segments of the population of Japan. When I made this decision, I was immediately challenged for my biblical basis—and rightly so. Many of my colleagues felt very strongly that the only way to remain true to the Word was the very opposite—to concentrate on the *un*responsive. Who was right? We turned to the Word of God, the final court of appeal.

No doubt the best way to begin a new movement is to do so under the stimulation of the Word itself. But if a movement arises or is developed through pragmatic innovation, through intuitive insight of a leader with charisma, or through scientific investigation, we have a double responsibility to uncover and examine the biblical foundation. This is true whether or not it appears successful.

Perhaps it would help to identify the background for this book. I speak as a friendly outsider to the Church Growth Movement, but as an active participant in church growth activity. For twelve years my privilege was to establish churches in Japan. For twenty years, including those twelve, I have been engaged in the study of what makes churches grow. When the Church Growth Movement began, I was naturally intensely interested. But my commitment to the authority of the Word of God compelled me to begin the long process of examining the new teaching in the light of Scripture. This book, then, is not the effort of a partisan advocate setting out to advance a movement, nor of an uninformed opponent with little stake in the issues, nor yet is it the musings of an unscarred theoretician.

Rather, these are thoughts that have been smelted in the furnaces of the Word, experience, research, and debate. They are offered in the hope that through this continuing interaction we together may more fully understand God's will.

In each chapter I will begin with a statement of the thesis (presupposition). Much of the controversy concerning the biblical validity of certain aspects of the movement has come because of imprecise understanding of the issue at stake. The presuppositions have often been assumed and left undefined. As late as the spring of 1972, McGavran said, "I have never stopped formally to answer the question posed by the title of this paper—What Is the Church Growth School of Thought?"[2]

Second in each chapter will be indication, through quotations, of the ideological confrontation. Simply to state all of the assumptions precisely and in logical sequence will not guarantee that the debate will hold to key issues. Even if the basic concept is clearly understood by those on both sides of the issue, a typical procedure is to pepper the opposition with prooftexts or biblical examples. We will stake out the battlefield with a few citations of these past skirmishes. This statement of the ideological confrontation will help to sharpen the issue, but something more is needed.

Next, the chapter will include isolation and examination of the theological issue. Only when we isolate the basic theological issue which underlies each presupposition will we be in a position to determine if the thesis is biblically valid. It will not be possible to examine exhaustively the great theological issues implicit in these theses, but the basic concepts will be identified.

The chapters will conclude with indications of any dangers or weaknesses of the thesis or of its application by practitioners of Church Growth methods.

1

NUMBERS

Is numerical church growth a most crucial task in missions?

Presupposition

Numerical church growth is a most crucial task in missions.

Confrontation

Church Growth people say:

> A chief and irreplaceable purpose of mission is church growth.[1]

> Fantastic increase of churches is obviously the will of God.[2]

> For the welfare of the world, for the good of mankind—according to the Bible, one task is paramount. Today's supreme task is effective multiplication of the churches in the receptive societies of earth.[3]

> God wants lost men found. He sends shepherds to find and bring home the lost. He is not pleased with token search. . . . When ninety-nine were safe and one was lost, our Lord commended the man who went out to search for it. How much more will He commend the man with one safe who searches for ninety-nine lost! . . . He is interested in the number of lost sheep found. . . . He wants a real finding of countable persons.[4]

> As soon as we separate quality from the deepest passion of

our Lord—to seek and save the lost—it ceases to be Christian quality.⁵

No numbers of redeemed persons are ever "mere numbers."⁶

Many oppose this sort of thinking, though for widely varied reasons.

Evangelical opponents make statements like these:

> We were not called to win men, but were called to glorify God.
>
> We are not called to success but to faithfulness. God is responsible for the results.
>
> Quality, not quantity, is our goal.
>
> There is one New Testament book on numerical growth, twenty-one books on spiritual growth.
>
> Remember the sin of numbering Israel—and remember the results.
>
> The New Testament pioneers seemed to be more motivated and controlled by the concept of taking the gospel to as many as possible who had not heard than by a drive to enlarge a group of churches as such, or even to multiply the numbers of churches.

Recently, some evangelical opponents say things like this:

> It must be warned that [McGavran's] system has become a new fad among evangelicals, a dangerous threat to the true, biblical growth of the church. It is a new version of the old Constantinism. . . . Should such Christianization be accomplished, the church would become little more than a "mass of baptized unbelievers." . . . "Church growth" responds to capitalistic presuppositions . . . the determining factor is not biblical teaching, but the influence of secularism. . . . The proclamation of the gospel (*kerygma*) and the demonstration of the gospel through service (*diakonia*) form an indivisible whole. . . . From this perspective, it is foolish to ask about the relative importance of evangelism and social responsibility."⁷

Nonevangelical opponents are also voicing views:

> To think in terms of church growth is to plan for survival, and this is the antithesis of the pattern of life laid down for us by Christ. . . . The Church's vocation then is to join in God's action in the world as He continues His movement of humanization.[8]

> The Church is not an end in itself. . . . In Him the whole of mankind has already moved into the new age which is the age of reconciliation and therefore a new relationship with God.[9]

> Throughout the Bible, the evangelization of the heathen is seen as a possibility only in the Messianic days . . . the Messiah is the evangelist . . . he will establish the shalom. And shalom is much more than personal salvation. It is at once peace, integrity, community, harmony, and justice. . . . This Messianic conception of evangelism means a total rejection of two very well-known methods:
> 1. It means in the first place a total rejection of everything that tends to be propaganda. . . .
> 2. In the second place, the Messianic conception of evangelism also means a complete rejection of another frequent misconception of evangelism. There is a stubborn tradition in our midst that interprets the aim of evangelism as the planting of the church (or even the extension of the church) . . . it is also true that planting the church in this institutional way of thinking cannot be the aim of missions.[10]

> The traditional western missionary outlook, that which is often expressed in the words, "go out into the world to preach and convert and plant the Church," was filled to the brim with western colonialism and imperialism. . . . Certainly we cannot deny that the traditional view of mission has been a religious counterpart to the military and economic imperialism of the West. . . . The missionary task of today cannot, therefore, be to draw men out of their religions into another religion, but rather to leave Christianity (the organized religion) and go

inside Hinduism and Buddhism, accepting these religions as one's own.[11]

If we take van Leeuwen seriously, our Christian concern is for the shaping of an authentic secular existence. We move toward the new humanity as we are free to live fully within history and work for the future of man. In other words, our concern as Christians is to have a secular rather than a Christian religious self-identity.[12]

The mission of the church in our time can be seen as . . . the management of the inhabited earth for its building up or development.[13]

We are not agreed among ourselves whether or not it is part of God's redemptive purposes to bring about an increasing manifestation of the Saviour within other systems of belief, as such. This very fact is one of the reasons which should make us leave it to the conscience and inner illumination of those who within other systems take up Christian discipleship, whether or not it is God's will for them that they should leave their own social, and religious community. The spirit of dialogue should anyway prevent our dogmatism on this subject.[14]

None of these texts [of the Great Commission], so modern scholarship tells us, gives an authentic saying of Jesus. It is rather an interpretative statement appended to the gospels by the Early Church about a generation later. . . . The borders of Christendom and heathendom, even between church and society, will have to be abolished. . . . Proselytizing is a non-Christian activity.[15]

THE THEOLOGICAL ISSUE

In this confrontation, the crucial theological issue lies in the field of ecclesiology, the doctrine of the church, and concerns specifically the doctrine of the nature of the church's mission.

To understand the mission of the church, perhaps we should first review the entire purpose of the church. This is especially necessary since so many in our day identify the mission of the church with the purpose of the church. By way of summary, through the use of analogy, let me list the purposes of the church as seen in Scripture:

1. The congregation is God's temple, where His people gather to worship Him and to keep His ordinances.
2. The congregation is God's family, to which His children belong for mutual care, discipline, and fellowship.
3. The congregation is God's school, in which His disciples hear and study His book.
4. The congregation is God's fold, to which His sheep are gathered for pastoral care, for counseling, and for healing.
5. The congregation is God's citadel, from which His soldiers are sent on missions of world redemption.
6. The congregation is God's service center, from which His servants go on missions of mercy to meet the physical, emotional, and social needs of men.

Is the congregation God's precinct ward through which His agents effect change in an unjust society? Israel was such an agent, but there is no New Testament evidence for such involvement by the church. Perhaps we could say that the congregation is God's shaker to dispense His salt in a tasteless society, to restrain evil and to promote good. But I find no injunction and no example either in Christ or the apostles that would encourage the church to engage in political activity. On the other hand, I see no principle or command that would prohibit the involvement of Christian men in political activity, and I see much that would encourage it. But the church, as church, is nowhere portrayed in this role. "My kingdom is not of this world," said Christ. Yet the Christian is certainly sent as the salt of the earth, and one who does not demonstrate concern for the whole man is not following the example of Christ.

Note that the first four of these purposes have to do with the ministry of the church to its own. Only two or three of these purposes have to do with the church's mission to those outside. The first four purposes could—and will—be accomplished far more effectively in the eternal presence of our Lord. But the mission of the church to those outside can only be accomplished during our earthly pilgrimage. Among these missions to those outside, does the Bible suggest any priority? Certainly the evangelistic mission is a chief and irreplaceable purpose of the church. I believe we can say even more than this statement of Church Growth thinking. More seems to be implied by Church Growth mood and activity. I believe obeying the evangelistic mandate is the crucial task in missions. On what theological basis do we make this claim?

World evangelization is the *expressed will of God*. By "evangelism," I mean proclaiming the way to life in Christ in such a way as to give men a clear understanding of this good news so that they may choose to become His disciples and a part of His church. By "evangelism," I mean persuading men, reconciling to God those men who have been alienated from Him, and bringing them into His family. World evangelization is the expressed will of God, both in the Old Testament and in the New.

In the early period of the Old Testament, when God selected a single people to accomplish His purposes, He was careful to indicate that His purpose was worldwide blessing: "And I will make of thee a great nation, and I will bless thee, and make thy name great; and thou shalt be a blessing: And I will bless them that bless thee, and curse him that curseth thee: and in thee shall all the families of the earth be blessed" (Gen 12:2-3). This passage was not incidental; nor was it isolated. God indicated this purpose repeatedly to Abraham and to his descendants (Gen 18:18; 22:18; 28:14).

Not only was God's purpose for the entire world clear at the beginning of His call to the chosen people, but it continued throughout the middle years. "God be merciful unto us, and bless us . . . That thy way may be known upon earth, thy saving health among all nations. God shall bless us; and all the ends of the earth shall fear him" (Ps 67:1-2, 7). "When the people are gathered together, and the kingdoms, to serve the Lord" (Ps 102:22). "Oh praise the LORD, all ye nations: praise him, all ye people. For his merciful kindness is great toward us; and the truth of the LORD endureth for ever. Praise ye the LORD" (Ps 117).

In the later prophetic period, the worldwide intent of God becomes even more clear. "It is a light thing that thou shouldest be my servant to raise up the tribes of Jacob, and to restore the preserved of Israel: I will also give thee for a light to the Gentiles, that thou mayest be my salvation unto the end of the earth" (Is 49:6). "Look unto me, and be ye saved, all the ends of the earth: for I am God, and there is none else" (Is 45:22). George Peters sums up the teaching of the Old Testament on missions:

> Universality of salvation pervades the entire Old Testament. It is not peripheral but rather constitutes the intent of Old Testament revelation because it constitutes the dominant purpose of the call, life and ministry of Israel. The Old Testament does not contain missions; it is itself "missions" in the world.[16]

If the Old Testament expresses God's will toward the whole world of men, the New Testament is even more clear. Again Peters says,

> To establish the theology of missions in the New Testament one simply accepts the New Testament for what it is. No reader can remain untouched by its missionary thrust and design. There is perhaps little theology of missions as such in the New Testament because it is in its totality a missionary theology, the theology of a group of missionaries and a theology in missionary movement. Thus it does not present a theology of missions; it is a missionary theology.[17]

"Even so it is not the will of your Father which is in heaven, that one of these little ones should perish" (Mt 18:14). Although this passage does not indicate the worldwide scope of God's will, it does clearly indicate that spiritual redemption is the will of God. Note that it is no blessing for one to hear and reject. In fact, it would be better not to hear at all. It was never the Father's will that the little one be fed, clothed, doctored, treated justly, and in the end perish. The New Testament is filled with clear indications of the will of God that men be redeemed eternally.

But what of the worldwide scope of God's intention? The key passages which indicate that world evangelization is the expressed will of God center around the Great Commission. In a recent gathering of missiologists, I suggested that "go ye therefore and disciple the nations" gives us an indication of the central purpose of missions. A leading missiologist immediately objected, "We cannot accept an isolated proof text as the basis for our thinking." However, the Great Commission is not an isolated proof text. This expression of the will of God is the major thrust of Christ's post-resurrection ministry.

On the evening following Christ's resurrection, He met with the frightened band of disciples and gave them the motive for their mission: "As my Father hath sent me, even so send I you" (Jn 20:21). At His command they went north to Galilee, and there He met them and gave them the method of their mission: "All power is given unto me in heaven and in earth. Go ye therefore, and teach all nations, baptizing them in the name of the Father, and of the Son, and of the Holy Ghost: Teaching them to observe all things whatsoever I have commanded you: and, lo, I am with you alway, even unto the end of the world" (Mt 28:18-20). The disciples returned then to Jerusalem. I see the events recorded in the last verses of Luke 24 as taking place at this time rather than before they went to Galilee. Here Christ gave His disciples the message of their mission, showing them in the Old Testament how it was prophesied "that repentance and remission of sins should be preached in his name among all nations, beginning at Jerusalem. And ye are witnesses of these things" (Lk 24:47-48). Our Lord then went with the disciples out toward Bethany to the Mount of Olives. They were still thinking of a political mission of restructuring a very unjust society, and inquired about the timing of Christ's earthly conquest. Our Lord came back to the same theme, "It is not for you to know times or the seasons, which the Father hath put in his own power. But ye shall receive power, after that the Holy Ghost is come upon you: and ye shall be witnesses unto me both in Jerusalem, and in all Judaea, and in Samaria, and unto the uttermost part of the earth" (Ac 1:7-8). We do not know the occasion of the most famous "Great Commission" recorded in Mark 16:15. But, assuming the events recorded in this disputed text are authentic, it may well have been yet a fifth occasion following Christ's resurrection in which world evangelization is expressed as the will of God, "Go ye into all the world and preach the gospel to every creature."

If a person is minded to question that this was the clear statement of the will of God, all he need do is examine the interpretation put on these commands by those who were present and heard Him. The disciples who heard these words left us thirty years of action demonstrating how they understood it, and the Holy Spirit considered it important enough to leave a book documenting that interpretation. World evangelization is indeed the expressed will of God.

Spiritual redemption is the *demonstrated activity of God*. It has been said that every act toward man after the fall is, in a sense, a missionary act. For example, revelation, or the giving of the written Word of God, was designed to bring men to Himself. The purpose of God's self-disclosure was not to make a proclamation or to vindicate Himself, but to save men.

The incarnation is pictured in Scripture as the great redemptive act of the ages. "The Son of man is come to seek and to save that which was lost" (Lk 19:10). "For God so loved the world, that he gave his only begotten Son, that whosoever believeth in him should not perish, but have everlasting life" (Jn 3:16). This is not a new activity on the part of God, breaking forth in the New Testament as a late innovation. It is seen throughout the Old Testament through the sacrificial system and the typology as the very warp and woof of God's purposes.

Even Pentecost is a missionary, redemptive act, according to the historian chosen to record it.

Evangelism and redemptive activity are expressed as the will of God and the demonstrated activity of God because it is the nature of God so to will and so to act. Love is the *revealed nature of God*.

In His nature, God is love. God did not decide to act lovingly after He created some object for love, but God from eternity was the great three in One—the Father, the Son, and the Holy Spirit, cemented in a relationship of living love. For this reason, God created man in His own image: to love and to be loved by a being designed on the same pattern. When man broke the relationship and thus damaged the pattern, God still, in love, reached out in redemption to restore man to fellowship and to the moral likeness in which he was originally created. That this is the essential meaning of life may be seen in the great commandment on which hangs all the will of God for man (Deu 6:5; Mt 22:37-40).

God loved the whole world of men to the intent that men not perish, not merely that they live and die comfortably. God, our Saviour, wants all men to be saved, and to come to the knowledge of the truth (1 Ti 2:4). For a man to be saved economically, socially, and physically in time and then to perish eternally breaks the heart of God, for God is love. There is joy in heaven over the sinner who repents (Lk 15:7, 10). There is great sorrow when he is rid only of his guilty feelings, but not of his guilt. There is joy when he is reconciled to God, sorrow when, even though reconciled to his fellow man, he remains alienated from God.

Again, God is not primarily interested in self-vindication, but in saving men, for He is not willing that *any* should perish (2 Pe 3:9). The Father's heart wants the prodigal to return, not just to know that he may. He wants lost sheep found, not just hunted. "He shall see of the travail of his soul, and shall be satisfied" (Is 53:11): the birth of sons into the heavenly family is all that will satisfy our God. God is love.

The salvation of lost men is that human event which *brings greatest glory to God*. Glory, in this sense, is the manifest essence of God or the revealed character of God. Surely the redemption and restoration of men puts His character on display as no other event. His love, His justice, His wisdom, and His power all are demonstrated in the restoration of a rebel sinner.

"Herein is my Father glorified, that ye bear much fruit" (Jn 15:8). The fruit of a godly character, called the fruit of the Spirit, is the redemptive work of God that glorifies the Father. Furthermore, the fruit of reproduction, bringing others into the family of God—"I have chosen you, and ordained you, that ye should go and bring forth fruit, and that your fruit should remain" (Jn 15:16)—brings great glory to God.

World evangelization is the expressed will of God. Spiritual redemption is the demonstrated activity of God. This is the expressed will of God and the demonstrated activity of God because love is the revealed nature of God. The salvation of lost men is that human event which brings greatest glory to God. This is the theological basis of the Church Growth Movement.

In summary, then, here are the crucial questions concerning the mission of the church:

1. Is evangelism valid?

2. Is evangelism a primary mission of the church, or is it a secondary mission?
3. Is the mission of the church primarily the redemption of men's souls for eternity or of men's bodies for time?
4. Is the mission of the church primarily the redemption of individuals or of social structures?
5. Does the mission of the church end with proclaiming good news, or must it include saving men?
6. Is the mission of the church the redemption of men in isolation, or of men in community, into the family of God, the congregation?

Church Growth people answer unequivocally: Evangelism is valid in our day and is a primary mission of the church to a lost world. The church's primary mission is reconciling immortal men to God and only secondarily saving men's bodies and societies. Though the church has the responsibility to proclaim the gospel to every creature, its goal must be to save men and not merely to inform them. The church is responsible not to save men in isolation but to bring men to birth into the family of God.

The Church Growth Movement is directly on target. Numerical church growth is indeed a crucial task in missions, including the number of people coming into the church and the number of churches constantly increasing. The evangelistic mandate is the primary responsibility of the church toward the world.

Furthermore, I believe that this is the greatest contribution the Church Growth Movement has made, bringing into sharp focus the issue of the mission of the church. The evidence also indicates that the movement has been very successful, probably the greatest influence in our day in causing many in the world of missions to reaffirm this basic biblical truth.

This does not mean, however, that those who object to this first great underlying presupposition of the movement, are wholly wrong, that no weaknesses or dangers exist.

Weaknesses or Dangers

When we bring the movement or its advocates to the bar of the authoritative Word of God, do we discover any essential elements of biblical truth left out? Are any extrabiblical truths held which are antithetic to revealed truth or promoted with inordinate dogmatism? Is the biblical balance askew?

Critics hold that, among Church Growth people, the evangelistic mandate is emphasized to the exclusion of other missions and other responsibilities of the church. Others hold that quantity and numbers have become an obsession to the neglect of quality growth in godliness. Spiritual growth is sacrificed to numerical growth. Are these valid criticisms?

First we must be sure that those who raise such objections are actually operating from the same commitment to the authority of Scripture. Also, we must be sure that such opponents are not doing what they accuse Church Growth of doing by overemphasizing the complementary truths. For their part, they must not overemphasize the social responsibility of the church toward the world nor the truth that spiritual growth is our first priority.

Having said this, however, we must admit the danger of neglecting our responsibility for showing mercy and seeking justice. This mission of the church must be fully discharged. Also it is apparent that some enthusiasts for church growth have neglected adequate emphasis on growth in godliness. Many, in zeal to save men (in the initial and all-important though limited sense of the word "save") and many in single-minded pursuit of measuring quantitative growth, have neglected qualitative growth. Such quality has to do with the ministry of the church to its own more than its mission to the world, but the two are integrally interrelated and mutually interdependent. For example, to work for or measure numerical growth of a people characterized by false living or false doctrine is to work for or measure something other than the true church, and so can no more be called quantitative church growth than it can be called qualitative growth. These weaknesses the movement must constantly strive to correct (see chap. 4 for a discussion of how Church Growth methodology may do this).

It is necessary to point out that quality and quantity are not intrinsically antithetical. "As soon as we separate quality from the deepest passion of our Lord—to seek and save the lost—it ceases to be Christian quality."[18] Numerical growth is not everything; it is not the only way to measure vitality, but it is *one* way. Numerical increase is normally one index of quality. Growth does not of itself produce spiritually weak churches. Ordinarily and ideally, each reinforces the other.[19]

One additional objection is often raised, that it is wrong to number or to count converts. Is this the teaching of David's experience as is often claimed? The time David counted the people, God told him to do so (2 Sa 24:1). Of course, it was for the purposes of judgment, and the chronicler says that Satan moved David to do this (1 Ch 21:1).[20] So the sin was there. But the sin was either one of pride and self-confidence or, less likely, of unbelief. Numbering the people of God and measuring results numerically is no sin. We have a book filled with such activity. It is, in fact, named Numbers.

The early church did not fear to count those who were being added to the church—three thousand, five thousand, multitudes both of men and of women, a great company of priests (see Ac 2:41, 47; 4:4; 6:1, 7; 11:21; 16:5). Indeed the whole book of Acts is response-oriented, not proclamation- or vindication-oriented.

In any event, statistical studies, though important in the Church Growth Movement, are not intrinsic to this first, basic thesis that numerical church growth is a crucial task in missions. One can work for growth without measuring it.

The central thesis of the Church Growth Movement, then, is built upon a deep, broad, solid biblical foundation. It is the response of men to the One who proclaimed, "I will build my church" (Mt 16:18). And He chose to do it through men, not angels. Because of false theology on the one hand and misdirected zeal on the other, God's great purpose may have been obscured in the middle decades of the twentieth century. But by His great grace there is growing a mighty response from the people of God; Amen, add to your church, O Lord. Build it through these poor instruments You have chosen. And the power of hell itself will not be able to resist our advance.

2

SELECTIVITY

Is it right for the church to concentrate on the responsive elements of society?

Presupposition

The church should concentrate on the responsive elements of society.

Confrontation

Church Growth people say:

> Support should be concentrated behind these growing, ongoing People Movement Churches. This is today's strategy.[1]
>
> Church growth as basis for policy might be stated in its "purist" form as follows: God's Holy Spirit in sovereign freedom prepares certain places at certain times for maximum receptivity to the Gospel; and evidence of this is given by the fact that the Church is growing rapidly. Our response should be to cooperate with the action of God by concentrating missionary resources at this point while the fruitfulness continues . . . or taking whatever other action is needed at this point to insure the maximum growth of the Church.[2]
>
> Only after the hundreds of thousands have been discipled is the world Church justified in spending treasure in witnessing to the millions of gospel rejectors.[3]
>
> Abandonment is not called for. No one should conclude that if receptivity is low, the Church should withdraw mission.

Selectivity

> Correct policy is to occupy fields of low receptivity lightly . . . they should not be heavily occupied lest, fearing that they will be swamped by Christians, they become even more resistant.[4]

Many mission thinkers oppose this principle of concentration on the responsive elements of society on three grounds: guidance, the Great Commission, and our service.

1. *The nature of guidance.* They feel that the Holy Spirit alone is an adequate guide and the only competent strategist, so the missionary task is to go where sent, not to anticipate the harvest. They reason further, saying that Philip was called away from a people movement and sent to one man; and the place of service is a matter of personal guidance by the Holy Spirit.

They also claim that the principle of apparently attempting to predict, in effect, how the Holy Spirit will work and how people will react on the basis of observed phenomena is based on the concept of uniformitarianism applied to the spiritual realm. If the validity of this principle is being seriously questioned in the physical realm, can we rely on it predicting how churches will grow and where resources should be deployed? As in the case of the individual, so with the group, present resistance to the gospel may only be a precursor to future reception.

2. *The nature of the Great Commission.* Here these opponents note that the Bible says we are to spread the gospel to every creature, a witness in each area, not many witnesses in some areas. Matthew 28:19 says *all* people; Luke 24:46-47 *all* the people; Acts 17:30: *all* men everywhere; Romans 1:14-16; 15:19-21: debtor to *all*. Christ by His example indicated that He must go on to the next people (Mark 1:37-38). They point out that the command is to the Jew first, and the Jew is ordinarily resistant.

3. *The nature of our service.* Their arguments are based on the following claims:

Our goal is not multitudes, but glory to God.

We are not called to success but to obedience.

The steward is judged by his faithfulness, the results are God's responsibility.

If God were interested in mere numbers, He would not have let Stephen be killed and John be sent to Patmos.

THE THEOLOGICAL ISSUE

Here the crucial theological issue lies in the field of soteriology, the doctrine of salvation, and is specifically concerned with the doctrine of election. The issue at stake is not the whole scope of election, but simply that element of election which deals with God's approach to man. Specifically, is God uniform or selective in His approach to men? If God is selective in His approach to man, on what basis is He selective; *why* is He selective? Does God intend for His agents to participate in that selectivity?

1. *Is God uniform or selective in His approach to men?* Although it is difficult for us to accept it, conditioned as we are through a prevailing mood of democratism, God has always been selective, both among individuals and among groups. It is true that He gives the light of nature and of conscience to all men indiscriminately (Ro 1:18-20; 2:14-15). However, depending on what response there is to that light, He gives or withholds additional light. As a matter of fact, for those who resist, God gives them up.

Christ Himself said that no man can come except the Father draw him; no man can come except it be given him of the Father (Jn 6:44, 65; 15:16). Romans 9 outlines God's selectivity in bold relief: "(For the children being not yet born, neither having done anything good or evil, that the purpose of God according to election might stand, not of works, but of Him that calleth;) it was said unto her, The elder shall serve the younger. As it is written, Jacob have I loved, but Esau

Selectivity

have I hated. . . . Therefore hath he mercy on whom he will have mercy, and whom he will be hardeneth" (vv. 11-13, 18).

In the Old Testament, God did not democratically choose the whole world. He chose Seth, Enoch, Noah, and, particularly, Abraham and his descendants. Without question, both the Old Testament and the New Testament teach clearly that God is indeed very selective.

2. If God is selective, on what basis or for what reason is He selective? No doubt there are reasons for God's selectivity which in His inscrutable wisdom will remain hidden to us at least until that day of fuller enlightenment in His presence. However, Scripture does indicate at least one basis on which God is selective in His approach to men. God is selective on the basis of men's response. To those who respond to the light they receive, more light is given. Those who are resistant have that light reduced or taken away.

Early in Genesis we read that God said, "My spirit shall not always strive with man" (6:3). This principle is seen throughout the Old Testament. For example, "Ephraim is joined to idols: let him alone" (Ho 4:17). "I will send a famine . . . of hearing the words of the LORD" (Amos 8:11). Israel was refusing to obey the light it had, so God was sending no further messages.

This is the message of Romans 9-11 concerning Israel. A hardening in part had come in Israel, and so the light was taken away.

This same principle is applied to the Gentiles in Romans 1, where it is repeatedly stated that God gave them up because they refused the light of creation. Knowing God through the visible things of creation, they did not acknowledge Him as God nor give thanks. Thus God gave them up (Ro 1:18-24).

Christ Himself operated on the same basis. He concentrated on the poor who heard Him rather than on the "righteous" unresponsive. "I came not to call the righteous but sinners to repentance" (Mt 9:13; Mk 2:17). Did God not love the self-righteous? Of course He did. But it was the sinner, the poor, the alienated who heard Him gladly, not the self-righteous and self-satisfied. Do we know that this is the reason for His selectivity? He said more than once that to the self-righteous He gave heavy ears and hardened hearts, for "whosoever hath not [a responsive heart], from him shall be taken away even that [opportunity] he hath" (Mt 13:12). Christ left unresponsive Nazareth because a prophet is without honor in his own country (Mt 13:57). He told His disciples to follow the same pattern, to leave town if the message was rejected (Mt 10:14), to flee if persecuted (v. 23).

In Luke 13:6-9 He gives a parable of the nonproductive fig tree which was to be cut down by the master's agent. Since this is a parable, we cannot build a doctrinal superstructure on it. But it does underscore the principle that God is indeed selective on the basis of response.

Why did Christ speak primarily in parables? He said that He used parables as a scrambled code to instruct those who were receptive, who had the key for decoding, and to obscure it for those who did not respond and thus did not have the key for decoding (Mt 13:10-16). He would not give precious things such as pearls to swine—that is, to those who could not properly use them (Mt 7:6). God is indeed selective. And one basis for His selectivity is very clear—the response on the part of those who hear.

But is this fair? Does the Bible throw light on the reason for this selectivity on the basis of response? At least some of the reasons God is selective on the basis of response are apparent in Scripture.

One reason for selectivity on the basis of response reflects the mercy of God. According to Luke 12:46-48, judgment will be based on the degree of light rejected. The more light rejected, the greater the guilt and punishment. For this reason God in love would spare the unresponsive from increased guilt because of increased exposure to light which they are rejecting.

Selectivity

A second reason in His selectivity of the responsive is not only for the sake of the unresponsive on judgment day, but for the purposes of their salvation now. The choice of responsive Abraham was, from the outset, a purpose to bless the *world* through him (Gen 12:1-3). God was working to save men of all nationalities, but He chose to do it through a responsive remnant.

Romans 9 is taken as a key passage for the doctrine of election, and the entire section of Romans 9 through 11 deals with the selectivity of God, rejecting Israel for a time because of its lack of response. However, the chief emphasis of God's sovereign election throughout these chapters is not so much His election of individuals to salvation but His election of instruments to effect His salvation. He elects people like Jacob and even Pharaoh to further His purposes of evangelism. "For the scripture saith unto Pharaoh, Even for this same purpose have I raised thee up, that I might shew my power in thee, and that my name might be declared throughout all the earth" (Ro 9: 17).

This truth is brought into even bolder relief in chapter ten, where we have one of the most magnificent missionary passages of Scripture: "Whosoever shall call upon the name of the Lord shall be saved. How then shall they call on him in whom they have not believed? and how shall they believe in him whom they have not heard? and how shall they hear without a preacher? And how shall they preach, except they be sent?" (vv. 13-15). Then chapter 11 spells out God's evangelistic purpose both in rejecting the unresponsive and in saving the responsive: "I say then, Have they stumbled that they should fall? God forbid: but rather through their fall salvation is come unto the Gentiles, for to provoke them to jealousy. Now if the fall of them be the riches of the world, and the diminishing of them the riches of the Gentiles, how much more their fulness?" (vv. 11-12).

The second reason for God's selective approach to the responsive is, then, that through them the unresponsive may be won. This purpose of God has actually worked out in history— the responsive have come, and through them those who are less responsive. Not only is this what God did with Israel and the Gentiles, but it is also what Christ did in going to the sinners, the poor, the outcasts who were responsive. Yet He apparently deliberately alienated the priests who were unresponsive, as indicated especially in the gospel of John. After multitudes of the common people had come in, Acts reports that a great number of the priests also were obedient (Ac 6:7). This is also Paul's pattern.

McGavran indicates that this is the result today, as well. He says that the best way to reach the resistant is to win the responsive first. Bishop Pickett reports that the only place in India in which any significant number of high-caste Indians have been won is Andhra Province where multitudes of outcasts were won first. Some missions worked for years among the high castes without results. When they finally turned to the low castes and won large numbers of them, they saw high-caste people come to Christ.

So it is clear that both of the reasons for God's choice to send more light to the responsive and less to the unresponsive are for the sake of the unresponsive as much as for the responsive. This selectivity means the salvation of more of the unresponsive now, and it also means a lighter judgment for those who remain unresponsive to the end.

3. *Does God intend for His agents to participate in that selectivity, or is this the divine prerogative alone?* Christ instructed His missionaries to shake off the dust of their feet if a town were unresponsive. This is precisely what Paul did repeatedly (see Ac 13:46, 51).

Take the example of Paul even further. Paul was not sent to all, but was particularly chosen as the apostle to the Gentiles. Did he go democratically to all Gentiles with indiscrimi-

Selectivity

nate evangelistic campaigns? Paul went straight to one segment of a community and concentrated on the winable or responsive of the Gentiles. He went to the synagogue and won the God-fearers especially. Paul did not even go indiscriminately to all the God-fearing Gentiles. He went to those living in the cities. Why did he do this? He does not say; and once at least he tried to go to a sparsely settled area (Ac 16:7) until the Spirit of Jesus turned him back. The Spirit of Jesus took Paul exclusively to the urban centers of the Roman Empire. This does not mean, of course, that the church is always to follow this pattern. But it does mean that God is selective for a purpose.

Paul did not even concentrate on the cities indiscriminately. For example, how long did he stay in what we might consider strategic Athens? What sort of work did he establish there? He spent years in Corinth and Ephesus. Do we have any evidence as to why he did this? He was to stay in Corinth, "for I have much people in this city" (Ac 18:8-11). In other words, God told him *why* he was to concentrate on Corinth—there were large numbers of responsive people there. What then of Ephesus? "But I will tarry at Ephesus . . . For a great door and effectual is open unto me" (1 Co 16:8-9). Paul concentrated on the responsive.

It is not accidental that Paul followed this pattern, for Christ on several occasions had given instructions concerning leaving the unresponsive. The same principle is in His command, "Give not that which is holy unto the dogs" (Mt 7:6). He was obviously indicating that His disciples were to participate in selectivity of approach. They were not to give truth to those who were unprepared to receive it and use it for good.

Although the passage on the keys of the kingdom (Mt 16:19) is highly controversial, the principle of human involvement in God's purposes of selectivity is certainly clearly enunciated.

Weaknesses or Dangers

I find nothing extrabiblical or antibiblical in this principle of concentrating on the responsive elements of society—the principle is thoroughly biblical. Nor do I find any teaching on the subject neglected by the leaders of the Church Growth Movement. They are at great pains to point out that responsiveness is not the only factor in deciding one's approach to a people. However, there is the danger that some may apply this principle in a doctrinaire way and come to an imbalance which in practice is wholly unbiblical.

This principle may be misused in two ways. First, it is quite possible in applying this principle to neglect a top priority in evangelism—saturation proclamation. A primary responsibility of the church is extensive proclamation. All men must have the opportunity to hear the good news with understanding so that they may consciously accept or reject God's invitation. But there are those who would, in singleminded pursuit of the principle of concentrating on the responsive elements of society, fail to "preach the gospel to every creature" (Mk 16:15; see also Mt 24:14).

Another danger is that some enthusiasts would program the church's resources right out of the less responsive areas of the world. They would apply this principle in a doctrinaire way, forgetting that in any given case other factors may enter and change the application. For example, God the Holy Spirit may know that great responsiveness is soon to appear in a given group. How tragic if none have responded to His call to be there in preparation for the harvest. Again, the Holy Spirit may have, for a particular individual or a particular mission, a lifetime of ministry among an unresponsive people such as most Muslims. The church as a whole must surely concentrate its resources on the ripe field, particularly since the responsibility for proclamation has been fulfilled to an unprecedented extent in our day. Yet forces to cultivate the fields

Selectivity 43

yet unripe are still necessary. Further, we need representative forces in the totally unresponsive fields to serve as outposts to vindicate the name of our God, to glean, and to reconnoiter for signs of life and response.

Those in positions of responsibility for deploying resources must constantly evaluate to make sure that the principle of concentrating on the responsive has not been misappropriated to foster either of these unbiblical emphases.

Yet the Word of God is clear: it is thoroughly biblical for the Church to concentrate on the responsive elements of society. God Himself is selective in His approach to men. This selectivity is based at least in part on man's response to God's approach. And there is no question but that God intends to use His missionaries, not only in the evangelistic approach but in the selectivity of those who should have the greatest opportunity. This is for the sake of the multitudes whose hearts have been prepared by God the Holy Spirit and who respond with joy to the approach of God. But it is also for the unresponsive themselves—for the salvation of greater numbers of them now through the witness of the responsive and, should they never respond, for a lighter sentence than they would deserve had they received and rejected more light.

3

CONVERSION

Are people movement conversions valid?

Presupposition

One desirable way for large growth is multi-individual, interdependent decision. This should not only be permitted but promoted.

Confrontation

Church Growth people say:

> Except in melting pots and individualistic civilizations, God has not worked that way (gathered individual approach) for 1900 years and is not working that way today. God has been discipling the peoples. For everyone out of a new people brought to Christian faith separate from his group, God has converted hundreds in chains of families. He has used the People Movement. That is the normal way in which the Christian churches have grown.[1]

Against this some opponents urge:

"Handpicked fruit" is best.
In our day one-by-one, man-to-man evangelism is the only way.
While a movement of the Holy Spirit resulting in the salvation of large numbers in a community, for example at Pentecost, is certainly desired, "people movements"

throughout church history have by no means always involved the salvation of the individuals of the group. Such mass movements must be spoken of with great caution, not held up as the ideal. The "people movement" begun by Constantine fares badly when evaluated by subsequent events.

THE THEOLOGICAL ISSUE

The crucial theological issue involved here lies in the field of soteriology, the doctrine of salvation, and is specifically the doctrine of conversion.

I discern no basic theological disagreement among those opposing one another on this issue, though a considerable lack of communication is evident. Earlier in the movement, statements were made which could only be rejected as contrary to the biblical doctrine of conversion as understood by most evangelicals. However, in the course of the years, such statements have been corrected so that the official, clearly enunciated position of leaders in the Church Growth Movement is wholly compatible with these evangelical convictions. When the term *conversion* is used to describe the same event as a person's new birth, all are agreed that this is certainly an individual matter. That is why the term *people movement* has been refined and defined, if not displaced, by the more precise term, *multi-individual interdependent decision*.[2]

God approaches and deals not only with individuals but with groups throughout the Old Testament, both for blessing (Gen 12:1-3) and for cursing (Ex 20:5).[3] The Old Testament makes a great deal more of group solidarity than does the New Testament, but it is clear from the Old Testament that God does at least sometimes deal with men in groups. That is, it cannot be said to be intrinsically immoral or unfair to deal with a group rather than with individuals.

Of course, even when God deals with groups it is always necessary for the individual to ratify the corporate decision.

"They are not all Israel, which are of Israel" (Ro 9:6). The people of Nineveh, from the greatest to the least, constituted a kind of people movement (Jon 3), but each, including the king, was called upon to ratify personally the repentance.

In the New Testament a clear shift to individual relationships is seen. But even so, considerable evidence exists of God dealing with groups. Of Christ's twelve disciples, a rather large proportion were Jesus' own relatives. Cornelius (Ac 10) and the Philippian jailer (Ac 16) are two prominent examples of households coming to faith as a group. Paul's approach to a city, not on an individual house-by-house visitation program but by approaching the synagogue (Ac 13:14; 14:1; 17:1-2; 18:4; 19:8) is certainly an approach to people who have a cohesion. Response was along the same lines.

If the basic issue is whether it is legitimate to utilize family and cultural lines or whether these must be disallowed on conscience, it is clear from scriptural example that an approach to the group is not intrinsically wrong.

Some people reject the entire Church Growth Movement because of misunderstanding this thesis. But others reject this particular thesis because of a misunderstanding of Scripture on their own part.

Most of us unconsciously tend to draw our evangelistic methodology at least in part from western individualistic philosophies, rather than from Scripture. As a result, some would question the sincerity of almost any decision unless it is validated by a clean break and open opposition to one's family and society. Such is often necessary and, when necessary, is clearly a test of genuine faith. Furthermore, when present, such courage is a highly praiseworthy attitude. But we must not extend this principle and make such a position the *sine qua non* of genuine faith. We are clearly unbiblical when we demand radical individualism, which is a western rather than a biblical concept. The cohesiveness of family and people and their inter-responsibility are strong emphases of Scripture. Yet many hold tenaciously to western individualistic concepts of conversion. Tippett gives a frightening example of this:

> Some Evangelicals still relate cross-cultural missions to their own Western conversion requirements. They cannot see a people movement as "under God." I have known some Western missionaries to refuse to harvest a field 'ripe unto harvest,' and even in one case to hold off people at gunpoint when they came as a tribe to burn their fetishes and thus demonstrate their change of heart. These missionaries wanted them to come one by one, against their tribal cohesion.[4]

Again, some raise the question of motivation. Should a missionary reject people who profess an interest when their motivation may not seem to be the highest? It should be noted that Scripture uses all sorts of motivation. Love for God is not a motive that can normally be expected of a non-Christian—it is a Christian response. However, fear and self-love are used constantly in Scripture as an incentive to draw people to Christ. How much more fitting it would seem to use as means to draw men to Christ the higher motives of love for family and loyalty to one's own people. Of course, to welcome people who come no matter what their motive must not excuse an indiscriminate acceptance into the church of unregenerate people.

Another objection has to do with the fact that the wrong ideas of a group are more difficult to filter out than those of an individual. To be sure, when large numbers from a single culture enter the family of God in a short period of time, many nonwestern ways will come with them. The foreign missionary may well be uncomfortable or have apprehension over the threat of losing control or becoming somewhat marginal to the main action. But we should not allow this to masquerade as zeal for the purity of the faith. We may be tempted to resist responsive people, controlling the rate of influx so that we have enough time with each individual to deculturate him and make him sufficiently western in his thinking and style of life to make us comfortable. But let us resist the temptation. The Bible is not western, and the pioneer evangelist must work uncommonly hard at the task of deculturating himself, not his prospective converts.

These objections make it clear that a people movement toward Christ has special problems—happier problems than massive rejection of the gospel, to be sure, but problems, nevertheless, which must be solved.

WEAKNESSES OR DANGERS

If the evangelist is open to the possibility of multi-individual, interdependent decision and is aware of the tremendous potential when such a movement begins, he will be very careful to permit and promote such a movement and not to stand in the way of the moving of God's Spirit. When such a movement is not in evidence, he will use methods which might make such a movement possible, not needlessly setting a man against his family or society and not introducing extraneous cultural patterns from the missionary's own culture.

When such a movement does begin, however, he will need to be cautious in three areas:

1. He must make sure that each decision is really genuine, that a live birth has actually taken place. The evangelist must not give a mass inoculation of spiritual truth that will effectively immunize people against the real thing. It is necessary to provide personal counseling with each individual to make certain that true repentance and genuine faith are present.
2. He must see that all who enter the family are well cared for. Tippett says that the failure in people movements has been more in follow-up than in the area of false decision.[5] This may be true, but who knows when birth has actually occurred? Who can be sure when the care ceases to be "prenatal" and becomes "postnatal"? The church or mission must provide continuous care of people before their

Conversion 49

decision, at the time of their decision, and, especially, following such decisions.
3. The evangelist must work ceaselessly with the leadership of the emerging church to develop spiritual maturity and biblical knowledge and understanding lest antibiblical cultural patterns come in along with those nonwestern ways which are biblically compatible (see chap. 4).

When the true issues involved are clearly focused, no theological reason hinders our pragmatic approach of accepting, with due safeguards, the findings of Church Growth people that point to the possibility—yes, the desirability—of large numbers of people coming to Christ simultaneously. When the evidence is clear that this means far more people coming into the family of God and at the same time evidence that those who come in this way are normally stronger in the faith than the typical individual man-against-his-people convert, it is indeed difficult to resist the enthusiasm of those who work hard at promoting the influx of tribes, castes, and peoples. The concept is especially welcome in this day of exploding populations that—apart from people movements—makes the task of world evangelization seem impossible.

No direct biblical mandate requires that we promote people movements. But there is nothing in Scripture against the acceptance of multi-individual decision. Indeed examples of it are found in the Bible. Furthermore, the biblical pattern is concentration on the responsive. And a ripe people-movement situation is the most responsive field of all.

4
SCIENCE

Are anthropological studies legitimate for evangelism?

PRESUPPOSITION

Anthropological factors affect a people's responsiveness. These should be analyzed and utilized.

CONFRONTATION

Church growth people say:

> A ... major emphasis ... is use of the principles of sociology and anthropology. ... By themselves these sciences are neutral. They neither favor nor oppose the expansion of the Christian religion. They are bodies of knowledge about how men behave. We believe this knowledge can be used to the glory of God and the expansion of His Church. We yoke these sciences to the missionary passion and use them in the service of the Great Commission.[1]

> The Church Growth School of Thought lays great emphasis on using the social sciences—anthropology, sociology, psychology—to aid churches and missions in bringing the nations to faith and obedience.[2]

Many evangelicals oppose this approach, claiming:

The weapons of our warfare are not carnal.
The arm of flesh will fail you.

Science

Do not rely on the horses and chariots of Egypt.

"Lean not unto thine own understanding . . . and he shall direct" (Pr 3:5-6).

"The seed sprouts up and grows—how, he himself does not know" (Mk 4:27, NASB).

"He that observeth the wind shall not sow . . . shall not reap" (Ec 11:4).

"Hath not God made foolish the wisdom of this world?" (1 Co 1:20).

We should not try to take the place of the Holy Spirit. It is He who must guide.

The Theological Issue

The crucial theological issue lies in the field of theology proper, the doctrine of God, and is specifically the doctrine of God's sovereignty and man's responsibility.

For a fringe of opponents a related concept may be involved —a type of dualism or dichotomy in which a great distinction is made between the sacred and the secular, and any secular or nonreligious element is disallowed.

However, for most critics the issue at stake, when pushed to its ultimate resolution, is the question of man's proper sphere of responsibility. Where does divine activity incorporate the human and when is it sovereignly unrelated? The same issue lies at the root of the biblical paradox of faith and works in salvation, the paradox of intercessory prayer and providence, the problem of election and evangelism. In each case it is far easier to run to a consistent extreme than to remain at the center of biblical tension. And yet, like the rubber band, such biblical truth holds only when in tension. We must not stretch our concept of the sphere of divine activity to the distortion of fatalism nor may we stretch our idea of the sphere of human activity to naturalism.

Is there biblical precedent for the use of human wisdom in doing the work of God?

When the children of Israel left Sinai, Moses said to Hobab, his brother-in-law, "Leave us not, I pray thee; forasmuch as thou knowest how we are to encamp in the wilderness, and thou mayest be to us instead of eyes" (Num 10:31). Moses promised to reward Hobab for this service, and Scripture records that God's people did not forget this promise (Judg 1:16-20; 4:11; 1 Sa 15:6). The passage in Numbers is remarkable because two verses later (Num 10:33) we read, "The ark of the covenant of the LORD went before them in the three days' journey, to search out a resting place for them. And the cloud of the Lord was over them by day when they set forward from the camp." Moses showed no hesitancy or embarrassment for this juxtaposition of the divine and the human.

Neither does Moses think it incongruous to receive the pattern for the tabernacle by revelation and then to seek out the most highly skilled men to accomplish the task.

The same thing took place when Moses sought to enter the promised land. He was relying on the instruction of God but at the same time he sent spies into the promised land. Of course, the research team members who had natural sight alone, who lacked the deeper insight of faith, were the ones who got them into trouble!

Solomon gave instructions to "lean not unto thine own understanding" (Pr 3:5). The entire book in which this gem is set is the strongest biblical exposition of what Solomon meant. He certainly did not mean not to *use* your own understanding, because a major theme of the entire book is to get wisdom and understanding (Pr 4:7-8). In fact, Proverbs' strong emphasis on common sense, on getting counsel, and on human wisdom is a large commentary on what "lean not" means and does not mean. It is the same balance we see everywhere else—do not *rely* on your own understanding, for it is ultimately God who will direct. But by all means *use* your own understanding for it is one way in which God guides you.

These examples indicate the way Scripture treats the whole

area of human responsibility. Man's responsibility to accomplish God's purposes here on earth is not set in opposition to the supernatural, to what God sovereignly accomplishes independently of men.

God is sovereign indeed, but in some mysterious way He has chosen to incorporate man's activity—prayer, evangelism, natural gifts, wisdom—into His sovereign plan. Since I hold this mediating view on the question of God's sovereignty and man's responsibility, I can wholeheartedly endorse empirical scientific analysis and utilization in the promotion of church growth. We are called to be good stewards of all our gifts, whether natural or supernatural. Tools have been given us in the twentieth century that have extended our bodies—the transportation revolution. These we use with gratitude to hasten completion of the Great Commission. Tools have also been developed that extend our voices—the communications revolution. These we use without hesitation in proclaiming the gospel. Tools have been developed that extend our time—the medical revolution. These we use with gratitude, keeping the missionary in service. Now tools are being developed that will extend our minds—the cybernetic revolution coupled with techniques of the behavioral sciences. Should we not use these also with gratitude?

Of course, these tools, far more than the others, have potential for encroaching on the sphere of God's activity. The mind, not the body, is extended. And herein lies both a unique opportunity and a unique danger. The mind is the image of the Creator, so that in putting our minds to His service we begin to participate in His own activity, whether creating or superintending His creation, or redeeming men. We do this at His command so that this is our glory—and His (Gen 1:28; Jn 20:21; 1 Jn 4:17; Mt 28:18-20). But it is also our great danger, for it is in the use of our minds that we are ever tempted "to be as God," usurping to some extent His prerogatives. Thus we advocate and use this Church Growth principle with the greatest care.

WEAKNESSES OR DANGERS

Three problems—two dangers and one weakness—are encountered when we bring Church Growth practice to the bar of biblical authority.

1. *The entire thrust of Scripture is on the supernatural, the divine in accomplishing God's purposes.* The Hobabs are a minority; human wisdom is constantly hedged. The danger of using these tools will be to change the biblical mix, to get out of balance, to give more weight to the body of empirically derived information than is legitimate on biblical terms.

We should not take Hobab out and shoot him, as a veteran missionary once told me. We should employ him. But we should not rely on him too heavily, or we shall be led astray. The danger is very real that in practice the computer with its programmer may tend to take the place of the Holy Spirit.

2. *The insights of anthropology, sociology, and psychology are normally used rather uncritically.* To use these uncritically is to invite disaster, for most of the presuppositions widely accepted in these disciplines are naturalistic. Psychology and sociology began as consciously antisupernatural, and all three disciplines retain large elements of the naturalistic mood and presuppositions. An antisupernatural bias would be bad enough in a field that was merely tangential to the basic concepts of biblical revelation. But in fact each of these three "soft" sciences deals with subjects that are of the very essence of divine revelation—the nature of man and his relationship to other men.

It is an all-pervasive and fatal error to disallow the divine dimension. Every idea about the nature of man and his relationships which is gained through independent human insight is almost certainly a distortion of reality. The insights of the behavioral sciences must be consciously and continuously integrated with revelational insights concerning the nature of man and human society. And in this integration when insights clash, the empirical yields always to the revelational.

Lack of integration with revelation is the greatest danger in Church Growth anthropology. For example, what in a culture may be retained by the emerging church? The Bible alone can answer authoritatively. Should Japanese Christians conform to the cultural pattern of ancestor worship? If they would do so, the churches would grow, we are told. Which answers this basic question of the Church Growth investigator—the science of anthropology or the Word of God?

The problem for the emerging church is extremely complex. Consequently, great diligence and uncommon wisdom are needed to distinguish the useful from the tainted. But such diligence and uncommon wisdom are absolutely essential if these scientific disciplines are to be put to the service of the gospel. Otherwise, the resulting mix will certainly be poisonous.

How are we to exercise this diligence? No evangelical anthropologist, sociologist, or psychologist would consciously build his thinking on antibiblical presuppositions. He is committed to the authority of the Word. Is this not enough? No, apparently it is not, for many evangelicals in the behavioral sciences have little more than a biblical veneer on naturalistic theory. What then is necessary?

The only way to reach an approximation of ultimate reality in the areas studied by the behavioral sciences is to *begin* with the Bible and its presuppositions and *then* to seek empirically for insights in areas to which biblical revelation does not address itself. To reverse the process and begin with the presuppositions and methodology of behavioral science and then to check with Scripture will do no more than add a bit of biblical flavoring to a thoroughly pagan prescription. One reason that abuse and error seem prevalent is that there are so few practitioners whose training has been in this order and of this proportion.

A spokesman for Church Growth thinking has said, "The character of missionary role has changed, but there must be a continuing missionary role. Now that the era of the old mission-station approach has virtually given way to a new era of partnership with, or fraternal-worker service in indigenous churches, there is no other feasible option before the Christian mission in communal and tribal societies, but that which is commonly called 'the church-growth approach.' The church-growth viewpoint is anthropologically based, indigenously focused and biblically orientated."[3] This is exactly what the movement often appears to an outsider, and this is what I fear. To be valid, the church growth approach ought rather to be biblically *based*, indigenously oriented, and anthropologically informed. Perhaps this is a problem more of semantics than of basic outlook, but church growth thinkers must be very sure that anthropological studies are not in practice the ultimate basis, or they will lead the church far astray.

3. *Not all the various factors affecting church growth are included in the research of the movement.* Does this adversely affect the validity of the research of those factors which *are* chosen for investigation?

Although it can hardly be said that this weakness is more significant than the two dangers listed above, it certainly is more complex. For this reason we shall devote more time to an analysis of the problem. But I emphasize at the outset that the dangers noted above more briefly are nonetheless more important.

If Church Growth practitioners do not investigate all the factors which affect church growth, what are those other factors?

At least five factors affect the growth of the church. Speaking in biblical analogy, the five are weather, seed, sower, soil, and sowing.

As factors in church growth, weather represents the sovereign purpose and activity of God. The seed represents the theological factor—the content of communication which is the

Word of God. The sower is the person of the communicator—the witness, whether he is professional and full-time or non-professional. Two factors in the sower affect church growth: the quality of his life (his character, the fruit of the Spirit) and the quality of his ministry (his calling, the gifts of the Spirit). The soil represents the receiver of the communication, either people as individuals or in a society. The sowing indicates the method of communication. All affect church growth.

Church Growth people concentrate on the soil (the receiver of the communication) and on the sowing (the method of communication). Church Growth investigation is also interested in one factor concerning the sower or the person of the communicator. It is interested in the number and the kind of "farmers" engaged in sowing and reaping.

Church Growth does not deny the other factors as affecting church growth, but some hold them to be more or less beyond the scope of scientific analysis. Again, some Church Growth leaders feel that men of God down through the years have concentrated on the other factors while neglecting the soil and the method of sowing. Therefore the special ministry of Church Growth investigators has to do with these two areas that have often been neglected. The neglect is not for theological reasons, and in many instances may not be deliberate. Dr. McGavran, for example, consistently stresses the divine factor in church growth.

> Although Dr. McGavran emphasizes the significance of the cultural factors which either stimulate or obstruct church growth, he is quick to recognize that the primary cause of church extension is the divine factor, namely, the operation of the Holy Spirit in the lives and affairs of men, recognizing the Church as a divine institution, not so much an organization as an organism.[4]

A. R. Tippett makes the same emphasis:

> You can take a Christian fellowship group and study it anthro-

pologically as an institution, and see "how it ticks" but if you carry your research to the ultimate conclusion you will have to admit that there is still one element which registers in your data but cannot be explained in human or processual terms. I call this the noncultural factor. It is, of course, the Holy Spirit. He is at work. Anthropologically I know how the church ticks, but another factor has to be introduced before the ticking is regulated as it should be. Given the current mood for religious change, and considering the missionary program in such a responsive population, I see no better way of handling the situation than by planting Christian fellowship groups that fit the local social structure and encouraging the people to pray for the gift of the Holy Spirit. If such a group is both indigenous in character and filled with the Spirit, and the religious mood of the location is innovative, we may expect a spontaneous expansion of the church. This is the regular pattern of people movements, and God has most certainly blessed it.[5]

Furthermore, recent efforts by leaders in the Church Growth Movement indicate a concern to see the neglect of the theological factor corrected. Yet in the face of this rather consistent historic neglect in Church Growth methodology, as a friendly outsider seeking to aid in the mutual quest for greater validity, I feel it is imperative to ask two questions.

The first question deals with the validity of such neglect. If the neglected factors in growth are ruled out as factors to be considered by this particular group of specialists, does the neglect invalidate conclusions drawn about church growth from the selected factors considered in isolation?

For example, it may be legitimate to study the biological sex factor in marriage in isolation from the affectional and spiritual dimensions. However, it would be a gross error to use the results of such a study as a prescription for a successful marriage. Studying the physical factor in isolation from the others invalidates many of the conclusions when they are marketed as a formula for across-the-board success in marriage.

In the same way, is it possible to really understand the receiver of gospel communication and the method of communication while ruling out a thorough investigation of the theological factor and the person of the communicator so far as the quality of his life is concerned?

In other words, *should* the other factors (the sovereign activity of God, the seed, and the sower) be neglected in Church Growth methodology?

The second question deals with whether they *need be* disallowed. Are these factors actually inscrutable? Since each is of a different nature, each must be considered separately.

GOD—THE FACTOR OF HIS SOVEREIGN PURPOSE AND ACTIVITY

The sovereign activity of God might seem to be inscrutable. His ways are not our ways. As the heaven is higher than the earth, so His ways are higher than ours, His thoughts higher than ours. Who has known the mind of God? Certainly this factor is not subject to scientific analysis.

However, this does not mean that the sovereign purpose and activity of God are totally inscrutable, nor that we need omit them in the study of church growth or nongrowth. For example, we may certainly discover indications in His Word and in His acts, as well as in personal guidance that shed light on the relationship between what He is doing or what He intends to do, and church growth. Furthermore, we can be involved with Him in this very factor in church growth through prayer. Of course, we may not be dogmatic in our conclusions about the sovereign purpose and activity of God unless the Word of God speaks clearly concerning His purpose.

Furthermore, we must constantly, consciously incorporate this factor in our church growth thinking because this is the *key* factor. God's sovereign purpose must always be the sentinel, standing guard at the door of entry for conclusions drawn from studies about the other factors in growth. If we do not check each empirical finding against the revealed will of God and hold it tentatively while awaiting His directions in corporate prayer, we quickly may fall victim to the very human error of absolutizing our method or our findings. Thus we open the door for error in our calculations. "Guidance by computer" is a dangerous but real possibility.

Church growth experience may have led Paul to aim toward the great metropolitan center of Ephesus, and irrational "spiritual" brethren may have taken the missionary band northward toward Bithynia. But it was supernatural revelation of the divine will that took them ultimately to Europe (Ac 16). This key factor in church growth—God's sovereign purpose—though it may be disallowed as an object of scientific inquiry, must be constantly incorporated in the practice of making churches grow. Prayer and the Word are still the greatest elements in church growth.

THE SEED—THE THEOLOGICAL FACTOR

Measurement of the theological factor may be difficult and certainly will have less than absolute accuracy. But it is not impossible, and it is dangerous to neglect incorporation of this factor as a major element in church growth data because many of the conclusions drawn from the study of the receptors of the communication, and of the method of communication, may be invalid if one has disallowed this factor of the content of communication as part of the investigation.

The theological factor and its relationship to the growth of the church is difficult because the problem is so complex. For example, a Christian who believes in the authority of Scripture begins a church and then is followed by one who denies the authority of Scripture. Does the growth or nongrowth in that church stem from the initiating work of the one who adhered to biblical faith or of the one who followed? Often the purity of the gospel presentation is given as a reason for the successful growth of a church. And yet, in a similar area where there is little growth, this same preaching of the pure Word may be given as the reason for nongrowth.

But to say that measurement is difficult is certainly not to say that it cannot or should not be done. Otherwise, evaluation of the receiver of the communication and evaluation of the method of communication would also be disallowed because they are so very complex. Of course, an investigator could study the growth of a church as a social group from a purely scientific perspective. Then we might more accurately call the study "social group growth" or "religious social group growth," in which case we would include Sokka Gakkai statistics along with the rest. This might be no more confusing than including statistics from churches that may differ as widely from biblical Christianity as frankly non-Christian religions.

But even in the study of non-Christian religions and their growth, we lay major emphasis on their "theology," or their values and concepts. We study how these affect men and consequently achieve or fail to achieve response in the particular culture or society in which they proclaim their tenets.

Actually, we do a great deal of this sort of investigation already. For example, for some years I studied the content of the initial evangelistic message as it relates to the Japanese value system.[6] This type of study is quite common and very valuable, often seen in Church Growth circles. It is frankly a study of ideology or of what we might call theology. But since it has to do more with the theology of other religions or the value system of a non-Christian culture, it seems to have been considered a legitimate part of Church Growth investigation, utilizing, as it does, the insights of anthropology, sociology, and psychology.

On the other hand, there have been several attempts at measuring the theological content of one's message as it affects church growth. *Christianity Today* has published rather extensive studies indicating how the theological stance of a denomination is correlated historically with growth and nongrowth.[7] More recently the widely acclaimed sociological studies of Dean M. Kelly have reached similar conclusions.[8]

In the light of this, would the conclusions of Church Growth investigation not be more valid and more credible if this basic ideological factor were openly included and much more greatly emphasized? Let the chips fall where they may. No one should think that the pure gospel message will always produce growth. In fact, this is the very thing that will hinder growth in certain contexts. However, this is the sort of information we need. When the relationship between the content of communication and response by the people is clearly understood one may use that objective information as his presuppositions dictate. He may change the programming of his communication, compensate for his handicaps, accentuate the effective elements in his communication. But only if he has that information. At least we will not be acting as if the content of the communication has little influence on receptivity.

Some say, "You're going to preach what you believe anyway, whether you get growth or not. And real growth comes only from sowing the true seed. So why not ignore the theological factor?" But is this valid? If I discover that Japanese are not responding because my presentation of the truth in irresistible Aristotelean logic is too logical to be true, will not such information help me to change my approach? Are there not emotive and intuitional elements in the gospel? Does not the gospel benefit a person? And if these are things which interest my hearer—though they may not interest me—am I not free to give him the truth which he desires and which he can hear with understanding? But how can I even know about this if the theological factor is disallowed as an object of study? On the other hand, perhaps it is the supernatural that is offensive. If Jesus is merely human there will be response, we learn. Does this information help me? Yes, for I can then understand the problem and work at the key issue of who Jesus is.

Again, needing to bring conviction of sin, must I work on convicting a Japanese man of the sinfulness of lying (which his culture does not concede), or should I use the sin of selfishness (of which he is acutely aware)? In either case, information about the theological factor in response is essential.

But is it legitimate for an evangelist to adapt his message to his hearer? Every evangelist adapts his approach for children and adults, educated and uneducated. But is not the message, the basic content, always the same? Jesus did not tell the woman at the well to sell all she had and come follow Him, nor did He tell the rich young ruler He must be born again. His approach to each person differed according to his need, as did the content of His communication. In fact, nowhere in the New Testament does any spokesman of the gospel—either talking to a person or to a group—give the whole package, the complete gospel message. The Bible messenger always spoke directly to felt need: need felt by the hearer, not necessarily the speaker. This need did not always lie near the surface of the hearer's consciousness. But the speaker in Bible history was highly selective among gospel truths, approaching each audience with a custom-designed precision message.

This does not mean it is wrong to tell a person immediately the whole story of his sinfulness, Christ's redemption and the way of repentance and faith, especially to one in a culture like America where there is a residuum of basic biblical knowledge. Nor does it mean we may leave out any essential truth in a long-term contact. But selecting message content in order to reach one's audience effectively is a thoroughly biblical way of doing it. Yet to do this, one needs knowledge of the relationship between his message content and response in the hearer. With such knowledge, the messenger can adapt the external form of his unchanging core message to reach the understanding and, hopefully, the motives of the hearer.

God Himself constantly adapts the encoding of His unchanging truth to the cultural context of those to whom He would communicate. The written revelation and the whole process of using men rather than angels as His spokesmen is an example of this. Those who spoke His Word also exemplified the principle, speaking in words easy to be understood—adapted to the language, culture, and understanding of the target audience. The incarnation is the greatest example of cultural adaptation for the purpose of communication. And Paul, the prototype missionary, deliberately sought to become all things to all kinds of people in order that he might win some of them.

Let no one use this principle to excuse compromising the essential message of the gospel. Cultural adaptation, as I use it, has to do simply with the form in which the message is communicated: the vocabulary, emphasis, timing, context, choice of cultural forms.

For two reasons, then, Church Growth studies and action must include the theological factor if the studies as a whole are to be valid. First, theological discrimination is necessary to validate statistical studies—what kind of church is it that is growing or not growing? Second, understanding the theological content of the message and the theology or ideology of the receivers of the message, and the way each affects the other is important for maximum effectiveness in communicating the gospel.

THE SOWER—THE FACTOR OF QUALITY IN THE PERSON OF THE COMMUNICATOR

Church Growth methodology constantly studies the person of the communicator so far as it concerns the quality of his ministry, his training, and the number of sowers. Visiting preachers on the mission field often concentrate, however, on the character of the person of the communicator, the poor quality of life of the missionary as the chief factor in failure to produce growth. But the quality of the person of the communicator is usually not incorporated as a factor in scientific Church Growth evaluation. Church Growth is interested in whether or not the sowers and reapers are present in sufficient number, and whether or not they are adequately gifted and prepared for the task. If sufficient numbers do not exist or if they are not sufficiently gifted, Church Growth investigation is very much interested in the question of training.

But are the witnesses godly people? Do they live supernatural lives? Although Church Growth investigators normally recognize the importance of godliness for church growth, they do not often program such investigation into growth studies. And yet is it valid to study the factors of church growth which are sociological in nature without considering these personal factors?

Are such factors measurable? A very extensive study by Ariga and T. Kosukegawa amassed a great deal of empirical evidence that such factors are indeed measurable. In 1967 a survey of 185 Japanese churches was conducted using three questionnaires: purpose in life; experience of conversion; and church life. A group of fifteen growing churches and twelve nongrowing churches were selected from the hundreds of participating churches. When the responses of the members in these groups were compared, a statistically very significant distinction in the quality of Christian life between the two groups became apparent in a number of categories.[9]

Tippett effectively uses church attendance as one measure of spiritual vitality and incorporates this "piety curve" in Solomon Islands Christianity as a key factor in church growth or nongrowth.[10] Certainly there are many other quantifiable elements that would give an accurate picture of this factor in church growth.

It is true that in a given context an unspiritual church may grow more than a spiritually strong church. But even this unhappy situation should be a proper subject for anthropological church growth study—surely isolating the reasons for the growth of a corrupt church will help.

I have outlined these dangers and weaknesses in the scientific methodology of the Church Growth Movement in some detail because I believe they are capable of being corrected. Note that they are in the area of methodology and not in that of basic presuppositions.

To the contrary, the presupposition that man should responsibly use the natural abilities and insights available to him in the service of God is so valid biblically that it should be extended to incorporate virtually all the factors which affect the growth of the church. To do less than this is to deprive Church Growth practitioners of vital information needed and also to jeopardize the validity of those areas which have been selected for investigation in isolation.

With these qualifications, we affirm that the fourth Church Growth presupposition, like the first three, is biblically valid. It is not prescribed in Scripture, so it lacks the same authority as that which is directly commanded. However, the biblical principle of using natural human resources in the service of God is clear. When used with care so that the emphases of Scripture are maintained in our method, anthropological factors indeed affect a people's responsiveness, and these should be analyzed and utilized.

5
PROPHECY

Will large growth result from using Church Growth principles and techniques?

PRESUPPOSITION

If these principles are followed, large church growth will often result.

Church Growth people say:

> At this very time ... the world (a mosaic of peoples) is much more responsive than it has ever been.[1]

> This amazing responsiveness is well known. Bishop Neill, the noted authority on missions, says, "On the most sober estimate, the Christian is reasonably entitled to think that by the end of the twentieth century, Africa south of the Sahara will be in the main a Christian continent" (Neill 1964: 568).... The movements of great populations lie ahead. The missionary movement has just begun.[2]

> For the first time in the history of the world, it is now possible (from the human viewpoint) to evangelize the world.[3]

> We are at the dawning of the day of missions.[4]

> As concentration of resources on growing points comes to be the strategy of missions, we shall find ourselves in a new era of advance.[5]

Opposition to this follows several lines:

"Narrow is the way . . . and few there be that find it" (Mt 7:14).

"Many are called, but few are chosen" (Mt 22:14).

The prophetic word emphasizes that there will be apostasy and an increase in evil throughout the age, but increasing particularly at the end of the age. There will be a remnant of faith only. "When the Son of man cometh, shall he find faith on the earth?" (Lk 18:8). These prophecies preclude the possibility of any large scale turning to Christ in this era before Christ's return.

In this scientific age of non-faith, there is no hope that large numbers will respond to a difficult life of faith in the supernatural.

THE THEOLOGICAL ISSUE

In this confrontation, the crucial theological issue lies in the field of eschatology, the doctrine of last things. A person could believe that large growth is possible but hold that *no* human strategy or methodology could bring such response. This theological issue concerning man's responsibility and God's sovereignty was considered in chapter four. Again, one could believe that large growth has come or might come or will certainly come, but not through the methods advocated by Church Growth people. This would then be a pragmatic problem, not theological. We would be free from theological inhibition and would objectively study the evidence as to whether these particular methods were effective in producing large growth.

But the chief opposition to Church Growth thinking at this point is from those millennialists who feel that no large growth is possible in this, the end of the age. The problem spreads somewhat when Church Growth advocates say things that sound postmillennialistic. When this happens many non-postmillennarians begin to feel uncomfortable even if they do not reject in advance the optimistic predications of large growth.

It would be far beyond the scope of this presentation even

Prophecy

to outline the case for each side of the prophetic issue. However, we may point out some implications of each position.

THE POSTMILLENNIALIST

The postmillennialist points to the prophecies which speak of "all nations," of God's universal intention; of parables such as that of the leaven and the mustard seed (Mk 4:31-32) which are taken to indicate the plan of God and the responsibility of the church to Christianize the world, to prepare a kingdom suitable for the King, and to welcome Him back to His kingdom. Many of the great missionary hymns, written in the optimism of the nineteenth century, imply that this is the task of the church.

> For the darkness shall turn to dawning,
> And the dawning to noonday bright,
> And Christ's great kingdom shall come to earth,
> The kingdom of love and light.
> H. ERNEST NICHOL

> Waft, waft, ye winds, His story,
> And you, ye waters, roll,
> Till, like a sea of glory,
> It spreads from pole to pole.
> REGINALD HEBER

> The morning light is breaking,
> The darkness disappears;
> The sons of earth are waking
> To penitential tears;
> . . . .
> Blest river of salvation,
> . . . .
> Stay not till all the holy
> Proclaim, "The Lord is come!"
> SAMUEL F. SMITH

The postmillennialist, singing lustily, has no problem with theories that predict large growth or total conquest. And many who are not overtly postmillennial in eschatology often tend to think in these terms. The danger is that people of this persuasion will fall into sinful pessimism because of the population explosion which increases the number of non-Christians in the world with every tick of the clock. Again they may be vaulted into foolish optimism by reports of whole continents turning to Christ.

THE PREMILLENNIALIST

The premillennialist believes, on the other hand, that the millennial kingdom will come only by the direct intervention of God at the second coming of Christ, and that only a minority of men will be citizens of His kingdom when He comes. It seems clear to me as a premillennialist that evil will increase, that apostasy will grow, that Satan has a program which he is bringing to a climax. But God has a program also. And He will certainly bring His great program of world evangelization to a successful conclusion.

His command was to disciple the nations (Mt 28:18-20). What the world will look like when the Great Commission has been fully obeyed and God's purposes for the era of the church have been accomplished, we do not know. However, in the light of the command, the church must assume that it has not completed Christ's purposes until every person has had an opportunity to hear with understanding the gospel and until disciples have been made, establishing a community of God's people, the congregation, in each locality. If one believes that God is at work in the world bringing this to pass, he views with glad acceptance reports of large numbers turning to Christ. No doubt the greatest turning to Christ in the history of the Church has occurred since World War II.[6] Although the wheat field is full of tares, God has prepared an unprecedented harvest of true wheat as well.

If one's theological position will permit him to be open to the possibility of large response, he then can examine the empirical evidence. Although I believe Christianity will always be a minority movement in the world at large, there seems to be no evidence in Scripture that precludes the possibility of a large proportion of any given society or community coming to Christ.

But even if this minority position were decreed of God for every community, and no matter how few are recognized as authentic Christians in the United States, for example, or in the Scotland of several centuries ago, it must be admitted that this number and proportion is vastly more than that which obtains in many communities around the world. So there should be ample room for growth on the basis of anyone's eschatology. For example, if church membership in Japan increased one thousand percent, less than ten percent of the population would be Christian. And that is a small enough remnant to fit through any eschatological narrow gate.

If a large response is ever possible anywhere, we are under moral obligation to aim for it. He is "not willing that any should perish" (2 Pe 3:9). He wills that "all men every where repent" (Ac 17:30).

Whether or not one believes that growth is possible has a great deal to do with his approach. Expectancy of response does not always bring results, because sometimes in our humanity we confound presumption with faith. However, nonexpectancy tends to guarantee little or no results. Nonexpectancy is a euphemism for unbelief. One thing growing churches have in common and little else. Growing churches are characterized by a great confidence that they can—no, that they *will* grow. They are churches that work in *faith*.

WEAKNESSES OR DANGERS

Church Growth people are incurably optimistic. This optimism is a tremendous boost to faith and no doubt has a great positive effect on missionary expectancy and evangelistic results, whether or not the theories and methods are all that the advocates claim. However, in this very optimism lies the danger that one will be set adrift from biblical realism. Though my theological position does not preclude great response sometime somewhere, nothing in Scripture supports the idea that large response will automatically occur if we follow some method. To have overconfidence in the method will predispose one to use it uncritically and to uncritically accept response and reports of response. If this takes place, the danger will then be to introduce masses of baptized pagans into the church.

On the other hand, should great growth not come, even though one confidently predicts it, he is being set up for frustration and disillusionment, or for self-deception or deception of others.

Whether or not Church Growth methodology will often produce large church growth, I cannot say with certainty. The movement is too young to yield empirical proof one way or the other. But some of the early returns look good, such as the people movement in the Christian and Missionary Alliance field of the Baliem Valley. But nothing in Scripture precludes the possibility of large response in times and places of God's appointment. Therefore, should not those who share Christ's compassion for the whole world and Paul's faith for its evangelization welcome these new insights on how we may more fully accomplish His purposes?

CONCLUSION

How Biblical Is Church Growth?

Is Church Growth thinking biblical thinking? Our brief study of the biblical basis of the major Church Growth presuppositions suggests that a uniform answer to this question is not possible. None of the presuppositions, rightly understood, need be in conflict with biblical teaching. However, only two were seen to flow directly from biblical mandate, two more seemed to be well derived from biblical principle, and one was seen to be extrabiblical, lacking both mandate and principle for validation. Yet even this was not seen to be intrinsically antithetic to biblical theology.

1. *Is numerical church growth the crucial task in missions?* Evangelism is indeed the crucial responsibility of the church toward the world. The church has other responsibilities, to be sure. The Christian, to be like Christ, must be concerned for the whole man, must work in compassion for the relief of human suffering. But the *great* commission is to reconcile men to God. This is the crucial task.

But is numerical church growth a legitimate definition of evangelism? Evangelism certainly must include the proclamation of the good news. Further, to be true evangelism, it must aim beyond proclamation to persuade men to accept Christ as Saviour and Lord. But it is more than proclamation and persuasion. True biblical evangelism has as its goal that new members be born into the family of God; that new parts be added to the body of Christ; that the number of Christians in the church increases. Numerical church growth is a startling but useful summary of this ultimate goal of evangelism.

This first, great principle of the Church Growth Movement is not, then, merely permitted by Scripture. It is commanded. Again, it is not an incidental command. It is the crucial command which indicates God's will for the church in His great purpose of redemption.

2. *Is it right for the church to concentrate on the responsive elements of society?* Here again, the biblical evidence is clear. God is selective in His approach to men and has consistently involved His representatives in that same process of selectivity. Responsive people, for their own sake and for the sake of the unresponsive, are always eligible for further light. Unresponsive people may, in the grace of God, continue to receive light. But, also in His grace, this light is normally diminished in proportion to the rejection of that light.

This Church Growth principle is second in importance only to the first. Like the first, it has ample biblical authority in the direct teaching of Scripture.

3. *Are people movement conversions valid?* We found no biblical mandate directing the church to seek people movements. On the other hand, we found nothing in the theology of conversion that would invalidate multi-individual decisions for Christ. In fact, we discovered ample biblical precedent for dealing with people in groups. Further, since a people movement is by definition a responsive element of society, this principle may be considered as a part of the second principle (concentration on the responsive) and therefore shares the scriptural foundation of the parent principle.

This principle of promoting people movements, which was the first to draw worldwide attention to the Church Growth Movement, probably ranks behind the first two in the overall contribution of the movement. It does not have the same biblical mandate as the first two theses, but it certainly has the validation of basic biblical principles and precedents.

Conclusion

4. *Are anthropological studies legitimate for evangelism?* For many people in the world of missions today, the use of scientific methodology and technology is the most prominent feature of the Church Growth Movement. I personally believe the greater contributions are Church Growth's clarifying the mission of the church and focusing mission activity on the responsive.

However, this does not mean that the scientific aspect of the Church Growth Movement is unimportant. Actually, all of the principles work together, reinforcing one another. The Church Growth Movement would change completely in character if any of the five basic presuppositions were omitted.

We found no biblical mandate to use the tools of science. We did find the biblical principle of using human knowledge and wisdom in the spiritual service of God, and we found some biblical precedent for this sort of activity. We found such activity playing a distinctly minor role in the teaching of the Bible, and we found the use of human wisdom in God's service to be carefully restricted. But the theological basis for using natural science was found to be thoroughly sound. Man's God-given responsibility to participate with all his finite resources in God's program need not violate God's sovereign will nor short-circuit His supernatural activity.

Biblical evidence, then, validates the use of scientific methodology in discharging man's responsibility to fulfill God's evangelistic purposes. But this factor will need to be used with caution in order to maintain biblical validity.

5. *Will large growth result from using Church Growth principles and techniques?* Although ranked in the fifth position, actually the entire movement would not make much sense if one did not presume that good results would follow the efforts of those who follow the presuppositions of the movement.

This principle lacks both a biblical mandate and clear biblical principle. However, we discover nothing in Scripture which would invalidate this conclusion. In other words, this is an extrabiblical theory, and as such deserves to be examined and tested pragmatically to determine whether or not it is true.

Such examination lies outside the scope of this study. And yet, inasmuch as Scripture does not teach that large response to the gospel is impossible and does affirm that God does not will that any should perish, Christians are under obligation to work and pray and believe toward large response. This brings us full-circle to the first presupposition that numerical church growth is indeed the will of God. If it is the will of God, certainly it is His will for us to use all possible means to reach His goal.

Is Church Growth thinking biblical thinking? Yes, it is. This is not to say that all the people associated with Church Growth think biblically in all applications and interpretations of the principles. But the underlying presuppositions of the Church Growth Movement rest on a solid theological foundation grounded in the Word of God.

These five principles should not be opposed because of a wrong application some mission thinker has made. Nor should they be the private domain of a group of specialists. These concepts about the mission of the church and how it is to be accomplished should be a moving force in *all* mission activity. These five Church Growth principles are indeed church growth principles—valid and important for the whole church of Jesus Christ.

APPENDIX

MILESTONE BOOKS IN THE CHURCH GROWTH MOVEMENT

By

RALPH D. WINTER

The list of books in this section is by no means exhaustive. The Church Growth movement derives from a broad spectrum of keen observers who have now and then, here and there, studied how societies are structured, how men and groups actually become Christian, how churches multiply, how movements to Christ are arrested or obstructed, and how evangelism develops. This is not the place to try to give credit to all whose thinking has contributed to the movement. Time would fail us to tell how Lorimer Fison, the Methodist missionary anthropologist, eighty years ago saw accurately the social structure of Fijian tribes and how this affected the growth of the church among them; how G. W. Vicedom explored the encounter of the church with the people of New Guinea; how Christian Kaiser, also in New Guinea, Bruno Gutmann in Tanzania, and Warneck in Sumatra wrote down observations in a similar vein. Certain writers did their work in some pocket of the mission movement so that their thinking did not contribute to the growth of the Church Growth movement until much later. Others' writings are not in English or are out of print. Our desire here is to list books which are immediately available so that readers can evaluate the Church Growth movement for themselves.

In any list of books on Church Growth, one is almost forced to tip his hat to William Carey's 1972 booklet, *An Enquiry,* as the first

---

This section was compiled and written by Ralph D. Winter, Professor of the Historical Development of the Christian Movement at Fuller School of World Mission and Institute of Church Growth.

statistical, historical, biblical, evangelistic, and organizational thrust that could be regarded to have set the pace for modern Church Growth studies. We look forward to its reissuance soon by the William Carey Library.

1910 to 1930

Roland Allen is the restless, indefatigable missionary, Bible-scholar, high-church Anglican whose writings almost single handedly in this period built up significant pressure for radical rethinking about missionary strategy. Not the same at all as the infamous *Rethinking* (1932) done by Hocking and others, Allen's works were highly spiritual and biblical but unfortunately did not gain a wide audience in the USA until the sixties, when with the help of Eerdmans, they splashed down as a triumvirate: *Missionary Methods: St. Paul's or Ours; The Spontaneous Expansion of the Church and the Causes Which Hinder It;* and *The Ministry of the Spirit* (selections from his writings), all currently in print, commented on below.

1930 to 1955

In 1933 *Christian Mass Movements in India* appeared, and its author, J. Wascom Pickett, immediately became a trailblazer for the study of group conversion phenomena in India. Later he became a professor of missions and the author of a second book to be mentioned in the next section. *Christian Mass Movements* is a book of 382 pages jammed with the data of real experience. McGavran, who shortly afterwards worked with Pickett in further studies, says that this book was "epochal" and "marked a turning point in mission history." "To leaders convinced that Christianization is necessarily a very slow and difficult process, Dr. Pickett's accounts of the triumphs of the Gospel . . . in the people movement fashion caused a revolution in thinking."

The collaboration of Pickett, McGavran, and Singh produced a second book in 1936, later to be reissued under the title *Church Growth and Group Conversion*. Echoing similar sentiments, and also in 1936, Latourette's prophetic world-wide summary *Missions Tomorrow* appeared, in which he wrote:

Appendix

> More and more we must dream in terms of winning groups, not merely of individuals. Too often, with our Protestant, nineteenth-century individualism, we have torn men and women, one by one, out of the family or village or clan, with the result that they have been permanently deracinated and maladjusted. To be sure, in its last analysis conversion must result in a new relation between the individual and his Maker —in radiant, transformed lives. Usually the group, if won, is brought over by a few of its members who have found, singly, the truth of the gospel and have begun the new life. Experience, however, shows that it is much better if an entire natural group—a family, a village, a caste, a tribe—can come rapidly over into the faith. That gives reinforcement to the individual Christian and makes easier the Christianization of the entire life of a community.

While this book is not available today, others of his are. Latourette produced almost one book a year during this whole period, including his seven volume *History of the Expansion of Christianity,* which elaborately investigates the spread of Christianity, the reasons why, the processes and methods, noting in detail the influence of the environment on Christianity and vice versa. In the introduction to the largest single volume he produced, *A History of Christianity (1953),* he spoke of "taking account of the forms of the faith which spread, the reasons for the expansion, and the methods, agents, and agencies through which the spread took place." (In 1963 he agreed to be one of the sponsors of the Institute of Church Growth, which McGavran had established in Eugene, Oregon, and in 1968, three weeks before his death in a car accident, he agreed to deliver a series of lectures on "European People Movements," at the new location of that institute in Pasadena, California.)

A significant development throughout this period was the growth of interest among American evangelicals in the concept of the indigenous church, much earlier advanced by men like Henry Venn and Rufus Anderson. Highly strategic was the decision of the Assemblies of God Foreign Department to pull off the field one of their most productive missionaries, Melvin L. Hodges, and ask him to blend his experience with research in what others were doing and thinking. The resulting book *The Indigenous Church* shows that he really did his homework, and it also shows the affinity between many different writers in different quarters. His book is peppered with references to World Dominion publications, to Allen's writings specifically as well as to Herbert Kane's, John Ritchie's, and to documents reflecting advanced thinking in the Conservative Baptist Foreign Mission Society. Moody for a time published a special edition entitled *On the Mission Field*. We will see this man again.

1955 to 1965

This is the period of initial institutionalization: the founding of the Institute of Church Growth at Northwest Christian College in Eugene, and the inauguration of the *Church Growth Bulletin* in 1964.

McGavran's *The Bridges of God, A Study in the Strategy of Missions* (1955) pulled it all together at that point in time. Latourette wrote the introduction. The book was published originally by the World Dominion Press, which in England had sponsored Roland Allen's writings, thus showing the affinity between the two. The same press came out with McGavran's *How Churches Grow, The New Frontiers of Mission* in 1959.

Presently the Roland Allen triumvirate of books mentioned above come booming in on the American scene, thanks to Eerdmans. *Church Growth and Group Conversion* also appeared again, reprinted from 1936, under this new title. Ending the period there appeared under Harper's imprint *Church Growth and Christian Mission* (1965) which brought under one cover four leading mission thinkers, from widely separated quarters: McGavran, Cal Guy (Southern Baptist, professor of missions at Fort Worth), Melvin L. Hodges, whom we have seen in the previous period, and Eugene Nida, that most widely travelled missionary in history, of the American Bible Society.

1965 to the Present

This new period begins with the expansion and reestablishment of the Institute of Church Growth. Now appeared the first fruits of a significant decision by the Eerdmans Publishing House—to start a

Appendix

Church Growth Series of books. Eight of the fifteen appearing through 1973 are reports of studies done at Eugene:

Church Growth in Mexico, Donald McGavran, John Huegel, Jack Taylor
Wildfire—Church Growth in Korea, Roy E. Shearer
New Patterns of Church Growth in Brazil, William R. Read
Church Growth in Central and Southern Nigeria, John B. Grimley, Gordon E. Robinson
God's Impatience in Liberia, Joseph Conrad Wold
Tinder in Tabasco, Charles Bennett
Church Growth in Sierra Leone, Gilbert W. Olson
Laity Mobilized, The Growth of the Church in Japan and Other Lands, Neil Braun

Another six have already appeared, which were studies done at Pasadena:

Latin American Church Growth, William R. Read, Victor M. Monterroso, Harmon A. Johnson
Understanding Church Growth, Donald McGavran
Church Growth and the Word of God, Alan R. Tippett
Man, Milieu, and Mission in Argentina, Arno W. Enns
The Philippine Church: Growth in a Changing Society, Arthur L. Tuggy
The Discipling of West Cameroon: A Study of Baptist Growth, Lloyd E. Kwast
God, Man, and Church Growth, Alan R. Tippett

Most of these are studies in specific regions, and all but two were done, at least in part, by missionary research associates rather than by one of the Institute's faculty members. The authors represent a wide spectrum of different church communions. One of the two exceptions referred to is McGavran's definitive work, *Understanding Church Growth* (1970), which is the best single book representing his thinking. A close second, of a very different type, is the volume which brings together the first five years of the *Church Growth Bulletin.* This is fascinating to browse through. More recently McGavran has edited *Crucial Issues in Missions Tomorrow* (Moody) and *Eye of the Storm* (Word).

This brings us to a second publisher that has begun a *Church Growth Series:* Moody Press. Five books have now appeared in this series: *Crucial Issues,* mentioned just above, *Historic Patterns of Church Growth* by Harold R. Cook, *The Unresponsive, Resistant or Neglected* by David C. E. Liao, *Frontiers of Mission Strategy* by C. Peter Wagner, and *People Movements in Southern Polynesia* by Alan R. Tippett, a profoundly significant work, almost half of which is devoted to general Church Growth theory.

The latter author, Tippett, produced two of the Eerdmans series as well, one of which, *God, Man and Church Growth,* is the largest, most comprehensive anthology of Church Growth writings yet to appear. His earlier *Solomon Islands Christianity* (1967) has set the pace for regional studies more than any other single-country study, displaying the full range of biblical, theological, ecclesiastical, historical, political and, above all, anthropological factors involved in Church Growth theory and practice. He has also given us *Peoples of Southwest Ethiopia, Bibliography for Cross-Cultural Workers,* and *Verdict Theology in Missionary Theory,* all of which are under the William Carey Library imprint.

The most recent institutional phenomenon in the Church Growth movement is the founding of the William Carey Library in 1969 and the Church Growth Book Club in 1970. The William Carey Library is designed to publish, whether by book, microfilm, tape, or film, materials that bear on the strategic aspects of the Christian World Mission. Its fifty-five books as of this date (1973) are too numerous to list. [You may request a list from the William Carey Library, 533 Hermosa Street, South Pasadena, Calif. 91030.] The Church Growth Book Club does not publish books but edits a section in each issue of the *Church Growth Bulletin* (which goes bimonthly to 8,000 people) highlighting books which it makes available (but does not send automatically) at a forty percent discount to subscribers. It stocks all the William Carey Library books plus more than one hundred others from thirty-four publishers, including virtually all the books mentioned in this article. Its larger list is available from the same address above. The club and the William Carey Library together have sold more than one hundred thousand Church Growth books in the past three years. This, in

Appendix

addition to the Church Growth books that have been sold directly by the various publishers like Eerdmans and Moody, is a significant measure of the present momentum of the movement.

Those who wish to follow the Church Growth Movement will also want to know about new ideas and new books as they constantly stream forth. Overseas Crusades has made this easy, and has put us all in their debt, by shouldering the publishing of the *Church Growth Bulletin* (Box 66, Palo Alto, Calif., $1 per year). It is edited by Donald A. McGavran and carries in each issue the section mentioned above on new books as they become available.

NOTES

Introduction

1. Donald McGavran, *Bridges of God* (New York: Friendship, 1955).
2. Presented at the American Association of Professors of Mission, Scarritt College, Nashville, Tenn., June, 1972.

Chapter One

1. Donald McGavran, *Understanding Church Growth* (Grand Rapids: Eerdmans, 1970), p. 32.
2. Ibid., p. 47.
3. Ibid., p. 49.
4. Donald McGavran, ed., *Church Growth and Christian Mission* (New York: Harper & Row, 1965), p. 244.
5. McGavran, *Understanding Church Growth*, p. 52.
6. McGavran, *The Bridges of God*, p. 97.
7. C. Rene Padilla, "A Steep Climb Ahead for Theology in Latin America," *Evangelical Missions Quarterly*, Winter 1971, pp. 102, 104-5.
8. J. G. Davies, "Church Growth: A Critique," *International Review of Missions*, July 1968, pp. 291, 294.
9. Marie-Louise Martin, "Does the World Need Fantastically Growing Churches?" *International Review of Missions*, July 1968, p. 312.
10. J. C. Hoekendijk, *Eye of the Storm*, ed. Donald McGavran (Waco: Word, 1972), pp. 46-49.
11. Kaj Baago, "The Post-Colonial Crisis in Missions," *International Review of Missions*, July 1966, pp. 324-25, 331-32.
12. M. Richard Shaull, *Protestant Cross-Currents in Mission*, ed. Norman A. Horner (Nashville: Abingdon, 1968), p. 98.
13. Paul Verghese, "On Prophecy and Technocracy," *Occasional Bulletin* (Missionary Research Library), October 1967, p. 6.
14. "The Kandy Statement," from the Consultation on "The Christian Approach to Men of Other Faiths," by the Division of World Mission and Evangelism within the World Council of Churches in Kandy, India, February and March 1967. Cited in *The Japanese Missionary Bulletin* 21, no. 4:236.
15. Marjorie and Cyril Powles, "The End of the Era: Further Thoughts on the Church and Mission," *Japan Christian Quarterly*, Winter 1968, pp. 38 ff.
16. George W. Peters, *A Biblical Theology of Missions* (Chicago: Moody, 1972), p. 129.
17. Ibid., p. 131.
18. McGavran, *Understanding Church Growth*, p. 52.
19. For a masterful exposition of this point, see Ralph D. Winter in *Crucial Issues in Missions Tomorrow*, ed. Donald McGavran (Chicago: Moody, 1972), 178-87.
20. For additional discussion, see Alan R. Tippett, *Church Growth and the Word of God* (Grand Rapids: Eerdmans, 1970). pp. 15-16.

Notes

CHAPTER TWO

1. Donald McGavran, *The Bridges of God*, p. 125.
2. "Church Growth Debate," *Church Growth Bulletin,* November 1964, p. 10.
3. Donald McGavran, "New Methods for a New Age in Missions," *International Review of Missions,* October 1955, p. 402.
4. Donald McGavran, *Understanding Church Growth*, pp. 229-30.

CHAPTER THREE

1. Donald McGavran, *The Bridges of God*, pp. 107-8.
2. See Alan R. Tippett, *Church Growth and the Word of God*, p. 31; and Donald McGavran, ed., *Church Growth and Christian Mission*, p. 73.
3. See Tippett, *Church Growth and the Word of God*, pp. 31-33. Actually the whole Old Testament parallels Eastern thought in general, treating the family and kinship groups as integral units.
4. Alan R. Tippett in *Crucial Issues in Missions Tomorrow*, pp. 84-85.
5. Tippett, *Church Growth and the Word of God*, p. 62.

CHAPTER FOUR

1. Donald McGavran, ed., *Church Growth and Christian Mission*, p. 239.
2. Donald McGavran, "What Is the Church Growth School of Thought?" (Lecture delivered to the annual meeting of the Association of Professors of Mission, Scarritt College, Nashville, Tenn., June 1972), p. 10.
3. Alan R. Tippett in *Crucial Issues in Missions Tomorrow*, p. 79.
4. John T. Seamands in *God, Man and the Church*, ed. Alan R. Tippett (Grand Rapids: Eerdmans, 1973), p. 95.
5. Tippett in *Crucial Issues in Missions Tomorrow*, pp. 99-100.
6. See J. Robertson McQuilkin, "Japanese Values and Christian Mission," *Japan Christian Quarterly,* Fall 1967.
7. Richard C. Wolf, "1900-1950 Survey: Religious Trends in the United States," *Christianity Today,* April 27, 1959, pp. 3-6.
8. Dean M. Kelly, *Why Conservative Churches Are Growing* (New York: Harper & Row, 1972).
9. T. Kosukegawa, report in *Japan Journal of Sociology and Psychology* 7, no. 2 (1968). In Japanese language.
10. Alan R. Tippett, *Solomon Islands Christianity* (New York: Friendship, 1967).

CHAPTER FIVE

1. Donald McGavran, "Ten Prominent Elements in the Church Growth Movement," mimeographed by McGavran.
2. Donald McGavran, *Understanding Church Growth*, p. 59.
3. Missions Advanced Research and Communications Center, from a talk presented at Inter-Varsity West Coast Conference at UCLA, December 27, 1968.
4. Donald McGavran, "Church Growth," lecture at Ben Lippen Church Growth Seminar, Asheville, N.C., July 1972.
5. Donald McGavran, *The Bridges of God*, p. 112.
6. See Ralph D. Winter, *The Twenty-Five Unbelievable Years* (Pasadena: William Carey, 1970).

BIBLIOGRAPHY

Selected Books About Church Growth

For those who have not read widely the literature of the Church Growth Movement and other work dealing with the growth of the church and would like to read selectively in the field, I offer some introductory bibliographic information.

Books on Church Growth Theory and Methodology

Understanding Church Growth by Donald A. McGavran (Grand Rapids: Eerdmans, 1970) is the most comprehensive statement of Church Growth theory by the leading spokesman of the Church Growth Movement. McGavran here puts together all the basic materials he has developed across the years and of which he has written in other books and many articles. It is a highly persuasive statement of church growth theory, and is at the same time a solid exposition of the basic reasons some churches grow and some do not, as seen by the man whose name has become almost synonymous with Church Growth.

A Manual for Evangelism/Church Growth by Virgil Gerber (South Pasadena: William Carey, 1973) is a primer of theory and especially of methodology in the Church Growth Movement. For the busy missionary or pastor who would like to understand and put into practice the basic insights of the Church Growth Movement but who does not have time to work through the more thorough studies and extensive literature, here is the book. For those who have read extensively in Church Growth literature but have not put it all together, this will serve as a good, simple, integrating statement. For any who would like to put Church Growth ideas into practice, here is a book that outlines the "how to" in simple language with clear instructions, samples, and materials.

Bibliography

Church Growth Bulletin, vols. 1-5, edited by Donald McGavran (South Pasadena: William Carey, 1969) are the first five years of the Church Growth bulletin bound and indexed for easy reference. For those who would keep abreast of what is happening in Church Growth and in the whole world of missions, this inexpensive bulletin is indispensable. (Write to Church Growth Bulletin, P. O. Box 66, Palo Alto, California. $1.00 per year.) If for no other reason, the review of all new books in the field will enable a student of church growth to be certain of keeping abreast.

REPRESENTATIVE CHURCH GROWTH STUDIES

The following examples of church growth studies, as widely varied as the entire literature of the movement, have been chosen because each is a unique representative of certain aspects or approaches to church growth theory and methodology.

Solomon Islands Christianity by Alan R. Tippett (London: Lutterworth Press, 1967) is the model for church growth studies. One of the hundreds of such investigations, Tippett's study remains the most thorough and comprehensive, covering virtually all aspects of potential investigation.

Latin America Church Growth by William R. Read, Victor Monterroso, and Harmon Johnson (Grand Rapids: Eerdmans, 1969) is an example of a church growth study that has had tremendous impact on missions, missions leaders, and the development of mission policy for a whole continent. A study that has been challenged from the right and from the left and has therefore become controversial, nevertheless it has uncovered basic facts that are changing mission policy and program throughout South America. This church growth study is an example of the impact such a scientific investigation can have and ought to have. The fact that most evangelical missions were operating without some of the basic information concerning the results of their ministry is a strong example of the necessity for this type of study.

The Twenty-Five Unbelievable Years, 1945-1969 by Ralph D. Winter (Glendale: Regal, 1972) is a missions history written through Church Growth eyes. For the pessimist who chiefly sees problems in the world of missions, this book is a real eye-opener.

What has taken place in evangelism and church growth since World War II is exciting and encouraging beyond belief.

Why Conservative Churches Are Growing by Dean M. Kelley (New York: Harper and Row, 1972) is a sociological study that pictures very graphically what is happening in the way of growth and nongrowth in the churches of the United States. The thesis defended ably in this book is that theological factors are determinative for growth and nongrowth in recent American church history. This book is an example, unlike almost all other church growth studies, of dealing seriously with the theological element in church growth.

BIBLICAL AND THEOLOGICAL STUDIES

Shaken Foundations, Theological Foundations for Mission by Peter Beyerhaus (Grand Rapids: Zondervan, 1972) is a powerful statement of the theological foundation of world evangelism. Beyerhaus deals very thoroughly with the theological issue of numerical church growth. This is a powerful answer to the liberal and predominate ecumenical view of the mission of the church. The objections to the church growth thinking raised in the July 1968 issue of the *International Review of Missions* and those raised by opponents of the Church Growth Movement in *Crucial Issues in Missions Tomorrow* (Donald McGavran, ed., Chicago, Moody, 1972) are authoritatively answered by this German theologian. A leading spokesman for evangelical missions, Beyerhaus was one of the chief architects of the famed Frankfurt Declaration.

A Biblical Theology of Missions by George W. Peters (Chicago: Moody, 1972) is without doubt the most thorough analysis of the biblical basis for missions. This is not a church growth book as such, but the theological issues dealt with in thorough biblical exegesis are often the theological issues raised by the Church Growth Movement.

ANTHROPOLOGY AND THE CHURCH GROWTH MOVEMENT

Bibliography for Cross-Cultural Workers by Alan R. Tippett (South Pasadena: William Carey, 1971) is for the serious student of the anthropological aspects of missions research. Tippett has prepared an authoritative and rather exhaustive 250-page listing of some 3000 books and articles.

HISTORY OF CHURCH GROWTH THINKING

Planting and Development of Missionary Churches, by John L. Nevius (Philadelphia: Presbyterian & Reformed, n.d.) contains the principles now known as "the Nevius Method." John Nevius originally gave the exposition of these principles in 1885. He made a break with traditional methods and advocated indigenous church principles. He believed in leaving converts in the occupation in which they were called and expecting them to evangelize friends and care for local believers without remuneration. The method was adopted by early missionaries to Korea and many have held that this Nevius method, with its concept of self-support, self-government, and self-propagation, accounts in large measure for the phenomenal growth and strength of the Presbyterian church in Korea. At any rate, Nevius' thinking had a great impact on the entire missionary enterprise, focusing on new methods that were held to produce greater growth and stronger churches.

Missionary Methods: St. Paul's or Ours by Rolland Allen (Grand Rapids: Eerdmans, 1962), along with *The Spontaneous Expansion of the Church and the Causes Which Hinder It* and *The Ministry of the Spirit* (selections from Rolland Allen's writings), have probably been more influential than any other writing in the changing methodology of evangelical missions. Rolland Allen's writings were strongly influencing missions thinking before World War II, but actually did not have their greatest impact on American missions leadership until after the war. He was a pioneer in challenging the old methods and advocating new methods.

The New Testament Order for Church and Missionary, by Alex Rattray Hay (Buenos Aires: New Testament Missionary Union, 1947) takes the basic concept of Rolland Allen, that the Pauline missionary method would be more effective than modern missionary methods, and works out a detailed and total methodology which uses the New Testament order as seen in Acts and the epistles as a blueprint for modern missionary work. This book had an uncommonly strong influence on American evangelical missionaries who flooded to foreign fields following World War II. In fact, it was the "bible" of methodology for many missionaries. For example, it was the first book published in Japanese by evangelical Japanese missionaries following World War II. This thinking controlled a great deal of missionary policy. Most of these policies have since been modified, as few mission leaders now believe that Paul's method can or should be used as an exact blueprint for every era and every culture.

The indigenous church movement, flowing from Nevius, Allen, and, to a lesser extent, Hay, combined with emerging political and cultural realities to provide the most important influence on mission thinking among evangelicals in the first two decades following world War II. Though the Church Growth movement which followed was to come at the problem from a different angle, indigenous church thinking had already conditioned mission leaders to raise questions about traditional missionary methods, to focus on methodology as a very important factor, and to insist on pragmatic evaluation of results.

SUPPLEMENTARY BOOKS

CHURCH GROWTH THEORY AND METHODOLOGY

Beaver, R. Pierce. *The Missionary Between the Times.* New York: Doubleday, 1968.

Beyerhaus, Peter. *Missions: Which Way?* Grand Rapids: Zondervan, 1971.

Beyerhaus, Peter, and Lefever, Henry. *The Responsible Church and The Foreign Mission.* Grand Rapids: Eerdmans, 1964.

Blauw, Johannes. *The Missionary Nature of the Church.* New York: McGraw-Hill, 1962.

Bradshaw, Malcolm R. *Church Growth Through Evangelism-in-Depth.* South Pasadena: William Carey, 1969.

Braun, Neil. *Laity Mobilized: Reflections on Church Growth in Japan and Other Lands.* Grand Rapids: Eerdmans, 1970.

Braun, Neil; Boxchman, Paul W.; and Yamada Takashi. *Experiments in Church Growth: Japan.* Miyazaki: Japan Church Growth Research Association, 1968.

Bibliography

Clark, Dennis E. *The Third World and Mission.* Waco: Word, 1971.

Edwards, Fred E. *The Role of the Faith Mission: A Brazilian Case Study.* South Pasadena: William Carey, 1970.

Hill, Leslie. *Designing a Theological Education by Extension Program.* South Pasadena: William Carey.

Hodges, Melvin L. *A Guide to Church Planting.* Chicago: Moody, 1973.

―――. *On the Mission Field.* Chicago: Moody, 1953.

Isaias, Juan. *The Other Side of the Coin.* Grand Rapids: Eerdmans, 1966.

Kraemer, Hendrick. *The Christian Message in a Non-Christian World.* New York: International Missionary Council, 1937.

―――. *Why Christianity of all Religions?* London: Lutterworth, 1962.

Liao, David. *The Unresponsive, Resistant or Neglected?* Chicago: Moody, 1972.

Lindsell, Harold. *An Evangelical Theology of Missions.* Grand Rapids: Zondervan, 1970.

McGavran, Donald A. *The Bridges of God.* New York: Friendship, 1955.

―――. *How Churches Grow.* London: World Dominion, 1959.

McGavran, Donald A., and Weld, Wayne. *Principles of Church Growth.* South Pasadena: William Carey.

McGavran, Donald A., ed. *Church Growth and Christian Mission.* New York: Harper & Row, 1965.

―――. *Crucial Issues in Missions Tomorrow.* Chicago: Moody, 1972.

―――. *Eye of the Storm, The Great Debate in Mission.* Waco: Word, 1972.

Neill, Stephen. *Creative Tension.* London: Morrison & Gibb, 1959.

Pentecost, Edward; Wong, James; and Larson, Peter. *Missions From the Third World.* Singapore: Church Growth Study Center.

Pickett, J. Waskom. *The Dynamics of Church Growth.* New York: Abingdon, 1963.

Pickett, J. W.; Warnshuis, A. L.; Singh, G. H.; and McGavran, D. A. *Church Growth and Group Conversion.* South Pasadena: William Carey, 1973.

Scherer, James A. *Missionary, Go Home!* New Jersey: Prentice-Hall, 1964.

Street, T. Watson. *On the Growing Edge of the Church.* Richmond: John Knox, 1952.

Tippett, Alan R. *Church Growth and the Word of God.* Grand Rapids: Eerdmans, 1970.

―――. *Verdict Theology in Missionary Theory,* 2d ed. South Pasadena: William Carey, 1973.

Tippett, Alan R., ed. *God, Man and Church Growth.* Grand Rapids: Eerdmans, 1973.

Wagner, C. Peter, *Church/Mission Tensions Today.* Chicago: Moody, 1972.

―――. *Frontiers In Missionary Strategy.* Chicago: Moody, 1972.

―――. *Stop the World, I Want to Get On.* Glendale: Regal, 1974.

Weld, Wayne C. *The World Directory of Theological Education by Extension.* South Pasadena: William Carey.

Winter, Ralph D., and Beaver, R. Pierce. *The Warp and the Woof, Organizing for Mission.* South Pasadena: William Carey, 1970.

Winter, Ralph D., ed. *The Evangelical Response to Bangkok.* South Pasadena: William Carey, 1973.

―――. *Theological Education by Extension.* South Pasadena: William Carey, 1969.

CHURCH GROWTH REGIONAL STUDIES

Bennet, Charles. *Tinder in Tabasco: A Study of Church Growth in Mexico.* Grand Rapids: Eerdmans.

Braun, Neil. *Laity Mobilized: Reflections on Church Growth in Japan and Other Lands.* Grand Rapids: Eerdmans, 1970.

Cox, Emmett. *The Church of the United Brethren in Christ in Sierra Leone.* South Pasadena: William Carey, 1970.

Edwards, Fred E. *The Role of the Faith Mission: A Brazilian Case Study.* South Pasadena: William Carey, 1970.

Enns, Arno. *Man, Milieu and Mission in Argentina.* Grand Rapids: Eerdmans.

Bibliography

Enyart, Paul C. *Friends in Central America.* South Pasadena: William Carey, 1970.

Gaxiola, Manuel. *La Serpiente y la Paloma.* South Pasadena: William Carey, 1970.

Grimley, John, and Robinson, Gordon E. *Church Growth in Central and Southern Nigeria.* Grand Rapids: Eerdmans, 1971.

Hamilton, Keith. *Church Growth in the High Andes.* Institute of Church Growth.

Hedlund, Roger. *The Protestant Movement in Italy: Its Progress, Problems and Prospects.* South Pasadena: William Carey, 1970.

Johnson, Alfred E. *Venezuela Survey Report, Potential for Revolutionary Church Growth.* Worldwide Evangelization Crusade.

Kwast, Lloyd E. *The Discipling of West Cameroon: A Study Of Baptist Growth.* Grand Rapids: Eerdmans, 1971.

Malaska, Hilkka O. *The Challenge for Evangelical Missions to Europe, A Scandinavian Case Study.* South Pasadena: William Carey, 1970.

McGavran, Donald, A. *Church Growth in Jamaica.* Lucknow: Lucknow, 1962.

———. *Multiplying Churches in the Philippines.* Manila: United Church of Christ in the Philippines, 1958.

McGavran, Donald A.; Huegel, John; and Taylor, Jack. *Church Growth In Mexico.* Grand Rapids: Eerdmans, 1963.

Mitchell, James E. *The Emergence of a Mexican Church.* South Pasadena: William Carey, 1970.

Olson, Gilbert. *Church Growth in Sierra Leone.* Grand Rapids: Eerdmans, 1969.

Randall, Max Ward. *Profile for Victory: New Prospects for Missions In Zambia.* South Pasadena: William Carey, 1970.

Read, William R. *Brazil 1980.* MARC

———. *New Patterns of Church Growth in Brazil.* Grand Rapids: Eerdmans, 1965.

Shearer, Roy E. *Wildfire: The Church in Korea.* Grand Rapids: Eerdmans, 1965.

Shewmaker, Stanford. *Tonga Christianity.* South Pasadena: William Carey. 1970.

Smith, Ebbie C. *God's Miracles: Indonesian Church Growth.* South Pasadena: William Carey, 1970.

Subbamma, B. V. *New Patterns for Discipling Hindus*. South Pasadena: William Carey, 1970.

Sunda, James. *Church Growth in New Guinea*. Institute of Church Growth.

Swanson, Allen. *Taiwan: Mainline Versus Independent Church Growth*. South Pasadena: William Carey, 1970.

Tippett, Alan R. *The Christian: Fiji 1835-67*. Auckland: Institute Printing and Publishing, 1954.

———. *People Movements in Southern Polynesia*. Chicago: Moody, 1971.

———. *Peoples of Southwest Ethiopia*. South Pasadena: William Carey, 1970.

Trevor, Hugh. *Church Growth and the O.M.F. in the Philippines*. Overseas Missionary Fellowship.

Tuggy, Arthur. *The Philippine Church: Growth in a Changing Society*. Grand Rapids: Eerdmans, 1971.

Tuggy, Arthur, and Toliver, Ralph. *Seeing the Philippine Church*. Overseas Missionary Fellowship.

Vought, Dale. *Protestants in Modern Spain*.

Wagner, C. Peter. *The Protestant Movement in Bolivia*. South Pasadena: William Carey, 1970.

Weld, Wayne C. *An Ecuadorian Impasse*. Institute of Church Growth.

Wold, Joseph. *God's Impatience in Liberia*. Grand Rapids: Eerdmans, 1968.

1182